Startup CFO

The Finance Handbook for Your Growing Business

Kyle Brennan

CONTENTS

INTRODUCTION

Having good financial management is critical to the survival of startups and small and medium businesses. Unfortunately, financial management is often an overlooked aspect for many entrepreneurs. This leads to an increased risk in a business failing due to financial constraints or unforeseen pitfalls.

It's intended that this book can be learning material for many different people and businesses, regardless of your stage or financial experience. We cover the basics of business finance and specifically how these functions apply to growing businesses. We also discuss the different focuses a CFO holds and how these roles help navigate the scaling of businesses.

1 WHAT IS A CHIEF FINANCIAL OFFICER?

A Chief Financial Officer is responsible for managing the finances of a company. But this general definition encompasses a wide range of duties and responsibilities. The CFO usually reports into the president and CEO, and they may eventually be promoted to take on these positions.

The key functions of a CFO include:

Comptrollership. The comptroller (also known as controller) is the officer responsible for a company's financial reporting methodologies and procedures. Their duties include oversight over the company's daily recording of financial transactions and the preparation of financial statements. The comptroller reviews financial statements to ensure their accuracy as well as if they adhere to the proper format and meet the appropriate standards mandated by government agencies.

On a daily basis, the controller is expected to ensure that all the money coming in and out of the company is recorded accurately. This routine recording work is commonly performed by bookkeepers under the controller's supervision, but in smaller companies, the controller may also perform bookkeeping functions. These functions include reconciling monthly bank statements, preparing checks and depositing money in the bank.

It is also the responsibility of the CFO to take this financial data and present it to management and other stakeholders of the company. The CFO has to ensure that the data is accurate since it will be the basis for many of the decisions made by senior management.

Treasurer. The Treasurer (also known as the financial officer) is responsible for overseeing the company's finances. As such, they are expected to be able to provide management with financial recommendations based on their knowledge, and analysis of, the company's financial data.

In addition, they are expected to monitor the company's investments and make recommendations as to where the company should invest its money. To more effectively perform this role, they may form and maintain relationships with investment banks.

In addition, the treasurer is also expected to prepare a budget showing the expected income and expenses for the coming years. If there are any special projects, the treasurer is also expected to prepare a budget for them, so that the company would know how much they would cost.

Since the treasurer has the best knowledge of the company's financial data, they may be tasked to talk to shareholders, as well as potential and current investors. They will talk about the business' current financial state, its financial targets and how it plans to meet them, and how it plans to stay profitable.

Economic forecasting and strategy. Since they have a deeper understanding of the company's current and historical financial situation, CFOs also take a role in ensuring its future financial health. In fulfillment of this duty, the CFO uses economic modeling and forecasting. Economic forecasting involves creating possible scenarios about where the company could be in the future in order to prepare any necessary corrective actions.

For instance, they can identify which of the company's operations are most profitable and help decide how to capitalize on it. They can also look at scenarios as to where the economy will be in the medium- and long-term. Using these scenarios, they can advise management as to what course the company can take in order to remain profitable under these economic conditions.

Other roles the CFO may take on include:

Risk management. CFOs may be involved in purchasing insurance for the company based on their understanding of its risk profile. For instance, they may recommend the company spend more on health insurance to reduce absenteeism of 'at-risk' employees.

They may also advise the CEO about risks the company is facing from legal issues within its industry and ensure that it adheres to current and upcoming regulatory requirements. For example, they may recommend that the company change its accounting procedures to meet new government regulations.

Stimulating the company's performance. The CFO may stimulate the company by providing advice as to how to innovate its products and services in order to remain competitive. They may recommend changes in existing products in response to changing market conditions. Or they may suggest new products in response to a market demand that is not being met by competitors.

They can also advise departments on issues of procurement, such as cost reduction and efficiency. For instance, if they believe that the company is spending too much on a particular good used in production, they may recommend looking for another supplier or renegotiating terms with existing ones.

In addition, the CFO may take on other functions such as ensuring the company follows operational best practices, overseeing employee benefit plans and taking on oversight over a company's acquisitions.

The CFO may also accept the responsibility of managing investor relations. They may present an overview of the company's finances during shareholder meetings to assure them of its continued health and profitability. They may also present a company's financial statements to potential investors to convince them that the business is a good investment for them.

Although Chief Financial Officers are commonly associated with larger businesses, these days small and medium-scale enterprises are increasingly seeking CFOs to help manage their finances. But the position comes with many challenges and risks that CFOs in larger corporations would not face.

For instance, the CFO is challenged to do more with the limited resources the company has. A CFO for an SME also has a greater range of responsibilities than one working for a large corporation, to the point where he effectively becomes a partner to the CEO.

Differences Between a CFO and a CPA

One of the most common misconceptions that many companies have is that they believe a Certified Public Accountant (CPA) can provide them with the same assistance as a CFO. In fact, they may even turn to their CPA for guidance on their business finances. While both CFOs and CPAs are financial experts, they have different specializations.

CPAs mainly focus on preparing a company's taxes using their knowledge of current tax laws. They should also be familiar with current and upcoming financial regulations to ensure that the company's finances are compliant with them in order to avoid legal issues with the government.

However, the CPA is not competent to provide you with advice on your financial strategy because of their limited viewpoint. Since the specialization of a CPA is in tax law, they can only provide you with advice from this perspective. They generally do not have a broad enough range of experience in areas such as corporate finance and operations to be able to give you the best strategic advice on achieving a business' medium- and long-term goals.

Thus, one key difference between a CFO and a CPA is in their focus. The CPA is focused mainly on the present, such as in creating the best tax strategy or preparing the company's financial records for an audit. The CFO, on the other hand, has to look farther into the future in order to ensure the company meets its strategic goals and maintains its financial health, as well as into the past, to identify trends that could indicate potential financial problems.

To illustrate, let's say the company is about to acquire another business. The CPA would advise you on the tax implications of the acquisition. The CFO would look at how the acquisition would affect the company financially and whether or not it would be beneficial in the long-term. They would also look at cash flow trends to see if the company could afford the acquisition.

Despite their differing functions, CPAs and CFOs need to collaborate for the greater good of the company. For instance, the CPA can provide insight on the tax implications of a particular situation to the CFO to help them make the best decisions.

Another question many companies ask is, do CFOs need to be CPAs as well? While it would be beneficial, it is generally seen as not necessary. Many CFOs actually start out on their career path by earning an MBA since it allows them to gain a wider range of skills such as marketing and supply chain.

It typically takes around ten years for a CPA or MBA holder to become a CFO. Once they are hired, they spend the first few years gaining experience in handling finances before they take other roles outside of this field, such as information systems, customer services and operations. When they have gained substantial experience, they usually become comptrollers as a prelude to advancing to the CFO position.

In recent years, however, fewer CFOs are staying long-term with companies and are choosing instead to seek short-term contract work. While this may not provide the financial stability of remaining within a corporation, many CFOs find it more rewarding as they are constantly forced to adapt to new situations.

The Importance of a CFO to SMEs

An increasing number of small and medium enterprises are realizing the importance of having a CFO. This realization has been made easier by the fact that it is easier than ever to hire a part-time CFO at a fraction of the cost of maintaining a full-time one as a staff position. CFOs can greatly add value to a company by helping improve their profitability and cash flow as well as the condition of their balance sheet.

What can a CFO contribute to your company? He can assess its financial health and help strengthen the areas in which it is weak. For instance, he can ensure that assets exceed liabilities. By having a strong balance sheet, you will be in a better position to compete for financing against other SMEs.

They can help ensure that the daily financial tasks of the SME are being done correctly. These include:

Internal reporting systems. This involves the creation of systems for creating financial reports that are generated for internal use. These reports are generally intended for management and the board of directors, and are prepared on a quarterly or monthly basis. They include the Statement of Financial Activities and the Statement of Financial Position and should also provide context as well as a one-page summary.

Financial reporting. This includes preparing external financial statements such as the balance sheet, income statement and statement of cash flows, as well as the notes to them; financial reports to government bodies such as the Securities and Exchange Commission; annual and quarterly reports for stockholders and press releases regarding earnings and related financial information.

Improving profit. A CFO can help a company increase its profit through methods such as suggesting pricing strategies, improving productivity and controlling costs.

Managing cash flow. The CFO ensures that the company has positive cash flow by ensuring that the net cash receipts exceeds cash expenses. He does this by putting a cash management system in place, which involves the process of collecting and managing cash and ensuring that it is allocated properly.

They can help a company with its strategic planning and set realistic and achievable goals. A strategic plan is a roadmap that helps a company achieve its goals. It involves four key elements:

Risk assessment. The CFO identifies the various risks a company faces and assesses them in order to prepare tools to help deal with them and avoid disruption to your operations.

Strategic planning. This involves a company defining what direction it wants to move toward and translating it into practical goals, as well as the steps to take to achieve them. It is different from long-term planning in that strategic planning begins by determining the desired end and then moving backward to determine what must be done to achieve it.

Timeline of implementation. Once a strategic plan has been created, the CFO creates a timeline to implement it. This timeline includes elements such as the tasks that need to be completed and a deadline for completing each of them. To ensure that the timeline is realistic, the CFO should have project management skills. For instance, he should be able to create a work breakdown that lists the deliverables that need to be finished.

Strategic review and exit planning. If you are planning to someday sell or dispose of your business, you need to create an exit plan. Your CFO can help you by determining the current value of your business so that you'll know what you can get for it as well as by creating various exit scenarios.

Even if you don't intend to sell your business in the near future, having an exit plan in mind will help with strategic planning. For instance, if you have a valuation for your business, the CFO can work with you to create a strategy to grow it to this level so that you can achieve your exit goals. The CFO can also inform you about the financial and tax implications of the various exit scenarios.

2 FINANCIAL REPORTING – WHAT FINANCIAL STATEMENTS DO YOU NEED?

When you are operating a small business, it is important that you keep track of how it is doing financially. For instance, are you making a profit or operating at a loss? How much money do you have available to meet your operating costs and daily expenses? Financial statements give you the answers to these and other important questions so that you can make informed decisions about financing, expansion and other vital issues regarding your business.

Financial statements provide important information about your business' financial health that you can use to determine its overall direction as well as identifying minor adjustments that you need to make. They are prepared using daily financial data that is recorded in your company's books, which trace funds going in and out of your business. Financial statements should be generated on a regular basis, generally once a month.

The three major financial statements commonly used are:

- The Profit and Loss Statement

- Balance Sheet
- Statement of Cash Flows

Profit and Loss Statement

Also known as the Income Statement, this summarizes your business's income and expenses over a given period so you will know how your business is performing. It measures your profit or loss using the simple formulas below:

Net Sales = Total Sales less Sales Commission/Discounts
Gross Profit = Net Sales less Cost of Goods Sold/Services Delivered
Net Profit = Gross Profit less Fixed and Variable Expenses

The profit and loss statement should be prepared regularly, usually every month or quarter and at the end of the company's financial year.

Costs are computed differently based on the type of business involved. For retailing and wholesaling businesses, the cost of goods sold is computed using the beginning and ending inventory as well as any purchases made during the recording period. For manufacturing, computing cost of sales is more complicated since you will need to look at raw materials, goods in process and finished goods inventories, as well as the costs of direct factory overhead and direct labor.

For service businesses, computing the cost of services delivered is less complicated since the bulk of your costs are the salaries of the employees actually delivering the service. For instance, your costs could include salaries, the fuel costs of the vehicles they drive and whatever supplies they use.

Here is an example of a profit and loss statement:

Profit and Loss Statement
For the Period Ending –
Amounts in thousand dollars

Income from Sales	45,000
Cost of Goods Sold	25,000
Opening Stock	20,000
Stock Purchases	10,000
Less: Closing Stock	(5,000)
Gross Profit	20,000
Expenses	12,000
Advertising	500
Insurance	1,000
Payroll	5,000
Professional Fees (Accounting, Legal)	4,500
Utilities	1,000
Net Profit	**8,000**

This is obviously a very simplified version of the statement, but when you actually prepare one for your business, it can be as detailed about the costs and expenses as you want.

Balance Sheet

This financial statement provides a snapshot of the business' financial health at a particular period (generally the end of the month or the financial year). It is divided into three categories:

- Assets. These are valuable items owned by the business including cash, buildings, land, furniture, equipment, patents, stocks, and accounts receivable (money owed to the business). They are divided into current assets, or those that can be converted into cash within 12 months, and non-current assets, which will take longer than a year to become cash.

- Liabilities. These are loans and other credit the business uses to fund its operations that are extended by external stakeholders. Current liabilities are those that must be repaid within 12 months while non-current liabilities can take longer.

- Shareholder's Equity. This is the amount of money placed by the owners into the business for use in its operations and to acquire assets.

The total assets should always equal the liabilities plus the shareholder's equity.

Here is an example of a balance sheet:

Balance Sheet

as of the end of fiscal year (FY) 20xx

amounts in thousand dollars

Assets

Current Assets	<u>28,000</u>
Cash	5,000
Accounts Receivable	20,000
Stock	3,000
Non-Current Assets	<u>70,000</u>
Office Building	35,000
Plant and Equipment	20,000
Vehicles	15,000
Total Assets	**98,000**

Liabilities

Current Liabilities	<u>40,000</u>
Accounts Payable	25,000
Credit Card	15,000
Non-Current Liabilities	<u>20,000</u>
Long-Term Bank Loans	20,000
Total Liabilities	**60,000**
Net Assets	<u>38,000</u>
Shareholder's Equity	**38,000**
Owner's Equity	28,000
Profit for the current year	10,000

Total Liab. & Shareholder's Equity   98,000

You can use data from the balance sheet to compute many financial ratios that would tell you how your business is doing. We will describe these ratios in the following section.

Statement of Cash Flows

This statement summarizes the flow of money into and out of your business. It shows where the cash is coming from and how it is used for a given period. It is also generally prepared monthly and at the end of the fiscal year.

It is divided into three categories:

- Operating activities. These are the cash flows that come from daily business activities such as payroll, income from selling of goods and services, payments made to creditors and payments received from debtors.
- Investing activities. These are cash flows that come from investments such as purchases of fixed assets and proceeds from their sale, as well as payments for stocks and other investments as well as the proceeds from them.
- Financing activities. These are cash flows coming from debt to finance a business' operations as well as debt repayments and cash injections by the owners.

The statement of cash flows can alert you to warning signs that indicate that your business is in trouble. These include:

- Your business is running out of cash (cash outflows are greater than inflows).
- Your net operating cash flow is negative.

- Your net operating cash flow is less than profit after tax.

Here is an example of a cash flow statement using data from the balance sheet and profit and loss statement.

Statement of Cash Flows
As of –
amounts in thousand dollars

Cash flows from operating activities.	28,000
Income from sales	45,000
Expenses	(12,000)
Accounts Receivable	(20,000)
Stock Purchases	(10,000)
Accounts Payable	25,000
Cash flows from investing activities	(70,000)
Payments for Non-Current Assets	(70,000)
Cash flows from financing activities	63,000
Increase in short-term debt	15,000
Increase in long-term debt	20,000
Owner's equity	28,000
Net Increase in Cash	21,000
Cash Balance at Start of Year	10,000
Cash Balance at End of Year	**31,000**

Tips for Preparing Financial Statements

Ensuring that financial statements are prepared on a regular and timely basis can be challenging for small and medium businesses that have limited staff. If you do not have employees with the experience and expertise to prepare these statements, you will have to train them and this can be a drain on your already stretched human resources.

There is also the risk of human error. When financial statements are prepared manually, there is always the chance that inaccuracies in reporting may creep in. These mistakes, no matter how minor they may seem, can have a major impact in the reliability of your financial statements. These can result in problems such as compromising your access to financing and affecting your credibility with shareholders and potential investors.

The best solution would be to outsource the preparation of financial statements to a CPA, but this presents its own set of challenges. You will need to find one that you can trust, since you are entrusting them with sensitive financial information. And of course, you would have to bear the cost of paying them; however, this can cost less than if you hired a full-time bookkeeper or accountant.

Alternately, you can invest in technology solutions that are designed to make preparing financial statements easier for small businesses. For instance, you can invest in cloud-based enterprise resource planning solutions that will automate your financial reporting. This not only ensures greater accuracy but also frees up human resources and gives you more time to focus on growing your business.

One advantage of using these solutions is that you can decide which financial statements are most important to you and set the software to run them as often as you need. If possible, you should create reports as frequently as possible, weekly if you can.

However, you may still need to manually fill in your financial data. While this routine task can be boring and time consuming, learn to think of it as an investment in your business. By ensuring that your financial data is accurate, you are actually saving time in the long-term since your operations will become more efficient and you have more accurate guidance for your business decisions.

3 USING FINANCIAL RATIOS TO INTERPRET DATA

Financial ratios are a valuable tool that allows you to analyze the data in your financial statements so that you would have a deeper insight into your business' financial health. As you learned in math class, ratios express the relationship between two numbers. To illustrate, let's say it costs you $20 to produce a product, and you sell it for $50, or a profit of $30. Hence, for every $1 you are spending, you are getting back $1.50 in profit, or 1:1.5.

Some of the essential ratios you should be familiar with include:

Common Ratios

These are the simplest type of ratio, and are basically computed by comparing them with the total to generate a percentage. For instance, computing the common ratio of your balance sheet would look like this:

Assets

Current Assets	28,000	38.57%
Cash	5,000	5.10%

Accounts Receivable	20,000	20.41%
Stock	3,000	3.06%
Non-Current Assets	70,000	71.43%
Office Building	35,000	35.71%
Plant & Equipment	20,000	20.41%
Vehicles	15,000	15.31%
TOTAL ASSETS	98,000	100.00%
Liabilities		
Current Liabilities	40,000	66.67%
Accounts Payable	25,000	41.67%
Credit Card	15,000	39.47%
Non-Current Liabilities	20,000	33.33%
Long-Term Bank Loans	20,000	33.33%
TOTAL LIABILITIES	60,000	100.00%
Shareholder's Equity	38,000	100.00%
Owner's Equity	28,000	73.68%
Profit, current year	10,000	26.32%

In the example above, the common ratio of the assets is computed as a percentage of the total assets, the liabilities as a share of the total liabilities and so on.

Computing current ratios provides a quick way for you to learn more about your business. For example, it lets you quickly evaluate the composition of your assets and liabilities. For instance, in the example above, if you computed the common ratio of your current liabilities, you would get:

Current Liabilities	100.00%
Accounts Payable	62.50%
Credit Card Debt	37.50%

This tells you that the bulk of your current liabilities comes from accounts payable, which can be money owed to suppliers, employees and partners, rather than short-term credit card debt. This means that, if you need to, you can push some of repayments on your payables to increase your current assets and earnings.

It also tells you about your cash position. In this case, your current assets are substantially lower than your current liabilities, meaning that will have to do something to boost your cash position or your receivables.

Liquidity Ratios

These ratios measure your ability to pay your business' obligations when they fall due.

Current Ratio = Total Current Assets / Total Current Liabilities

The current ratio is a measure of the business' financial strength. It looks at if your business has enough current assets to meet your short-term obligations (those payable within a year) while still maintaining a sufficient amount of cash as a safety buffer.

An acceptable current ratio is 2:1, but this would depend on what industry your business is in and what form of your assets and liabilities are in. For instance, if your assets are heavily liquid (i.e. cash) your business can survive

21

with a lower ratio. Generally, however, the higher the current ratio, the better.

Quick Ratio = (Current Assets less Inventory) / (Current Liabilities less Overdraft)

This ratio is also known as the Acid Test Ratio and measures liquidity by focusing on assets that can easily be converted into cash. It does this by excluding inventory since it might take some time before these goods can be sold. It helps address the question: could you still meet your pending obligations if you only have funds on hand and do not receive any income for a certain period?

Solvency Ratios

These ratios answer the question: with reduced cash flow, will the business be able to meet its current obligations using other sources? The ratios most commonly used are:

Leverage Ratio = Total Liabilities / Total Equity

Note: equity is computed as Net Assets less Net Liabilities. This ratio measures how reliant the business is on debt to finance its business rather than equity. The higher the leverage ratio, the harder it will be for the business to borrow further in the future.

Debt to Assets = Total Liabilities / Total Assets

This ratio measures what percentage of your assets is financed using liabilities. In general, the debt-to-assets ratio should be below 1 since it shows that you have sufficient assets in order to finance all your debt.

To illustrate how these two ratios can help assess a company's financial condition, let us analyze the balance sheet of our hypothetical business.

Using financial data from the balance sheet, we get the following ratios:

Current Ratio = 0.7
Quick Ratio = 0.63
Debt to Equity = 1.58
Debt to Assets = 0.61

Unfortunately, these ratios paint a picture of a company that is in poor financial health. Its current ratio indicates that only $0.70 of current assets are available to cover $1 of current liabilities. Its quick ratio paints an even more dire picture, with only $0.63 of liquid assets for every $1 of current liabilities.

Its debt to equity ratio shows that debt exceeds equity by 1.5 times, while two-thirds of the company's assets have been financed by debt. This means that if the company suddenly had a cash-flow problem, even a short-term one, it would be difficult to meet current obligations such as payroll and debt payments.

Normally, a company would be able to withstand such a crisis through a liquidity injection, such as through a bank loan. Alternately, it could liquidate or pledge some of its assets to generate liquidity.

But if a company is insolvent, i.e. it does not have enough liquid assets to generate cash to meet is obligations, then it may need to take action to reduce its costs. This may require the company to start pursing its accounts receivable to generate cash or more drastic moves such as laying-off workers or reducing its operations.

Profitability Ratios

These ratios will tell you how successful your business is by measuring its performance. They will show how effectively a company utilizes its assets to generate profit relative to its income, shareholder's equity, operating costs and assets in its balance sheet.

Gross Margin Ratio = Gross Profit / Net Income

This ratio measures what percentage of your sales is left (after the cost of manufacturing or buying goods sold is deducted) to meet your business' overhead expenses.

Net Margin Ratio = Net Profit / Net Income

This ratio measures what percentage of sales remain after all expenses (except income taxes) have been deducted. It allows you to assess your business' performance by looking at its return on income, and lets you compare it with other businesses.

Management Ratios

These ratios are a measure of how you manage your working capital so that you can improve your business' performance. They also allow you to assess your business by measuring it against industry averages.

Days Inventory = Inventory / Cost of Goods Sold X 365

This ratio indicates how quickly you are replacing your stock, and is a measure of profitability. The more frequent your inventory turnover, the more profitable your business is.

To illustrate, let's say that:

Inventory = $2,320
Cost of Goods Sold = $21,300

Your Days Inventory is 39.76 days

Days Debtors = Accounts Receivable / Net Sales X 365

This ratio measures your business' liquidity by looking at how well you are collecting your accounts receivable.

Thus, if:

Receivables = $3,450
Net Sales = $32,500

Your Days Debtors is 38.75 days

Days Creditors = Accounts Payable / Cost of Goods Sold X 365

This ratio looks at how effective your business' cash flow is by examining how you manage your accounts payable. For instance, if on average you are settling your payables before your agreed payment terms or before you have collected debts, it may affect your cash flows.

Example:

Accounts Payable = $1,210
Cost of Goods Sold = $11,564

Your Days Creditors is 38.2 days

Balance Sheet Ratios

These ratios measure how effectively your business is making a profit by using its assets and equity.

Return on Assets = Net Profit Before Tax / Total Assets X 100

This ratio measures how efficiently you are using your assets in your business to generate profits. However, it is meaningful only if you measure it against industry averages or the ratios of other businesses in your industry. Having a low ratio compared with others' indicates that you are using your assets inefficiently.

Return on Investment = Net Profit Before Tax / Equity X 100

This ratio tells you if the investment in your business is worth it. Your ROI indicates if you are generating a suitable return relative to the equity you put in it.

Using Ratios to Perform a Financial Analysis of Your Business

While current financial ratios can be instructive in giving you a picture of where your business is at now, they are not enough to give you a full idea of the financial health of your business. To do that, you need to create a basis for comparison.

The first basis is the past performance of your company. This means that you have to compute financial ratios for at least the past three years, or even further back if older financial data is available. Doing this will tell you if your financial condition is doing better or worse.

It also helps you to identify trends that indicate adjustments may be necessary. For instance, if your liquidity has been declining over the past few years you can make adjustments before the problem becomes too serious.

The second basis is how your competitors are performing. While you may be satisfied if your company is growing 15% annually, if your competitors are growing by 25% then it indicates that your business is underperforming.

Financial ratios also tell you if you are meeting your obligations. For instance, if your shareholders require you to hit certain benchmarks for financial performance, financial ratios can tell you if you are meeting them.

4 HOW CASH MANAGEMENT ENSURES YOUR BUSINESS' SURVIVAL

Effectively managing cash spells the difference between success and failure for small and medium businesses. Having a regular supply of cash not only means that a business can meet its current obligation but also has enough capital to fund future growth. Having enough cash on hand also means that a company can survive for a while if it suddenly suffers from liquidity problems or cash outflow issues.

There are essentially two types of cash flows:

- Positive. You experience these cash flows when inflow from accounts receivables and sales exceed outflows through regular expenses, payroll and accounts payable.
- Negative. This occurs when the cash outflows exceed inflows, such as if your costs exceed your sales. This can cause liquidity problems if a business finds that it does not have enough cash on hand to meet its obligations.

In the past, small businesses would deal with liquidity problems by seeking short-term financing from lending sources or availing of a bank overdraft. In recent years, however, it has become harder for SMEs to obtain credit due to the perception they represent a higher lending risk as well as a lack of transparency. As a result, many small businesses are suffering from a cash crunch, which makes it more difficult for them to meet their current obligations, much less finance future growth.

Signs that a business is experiencing poor cash management include:

- Inability to service debt and meet current liabilities due to recurring cash shortages
- Inability to acquire financing for operating capital
- Lack of controls over receivables, payables and inventories
- Lack of clarity over requirements for short-term cash
- Lack of plans for generating cash internally

Here are some of the steps a company can take in order to create a comprehensive cash management process:

Develop a rolling cash forecast. This lays out your estimated monthly cash payments and receipts for the coming year. The purpose of creating this forecast is to be able to foresee potential cash flow problems in the future and create plans to manage them now. Details on how to create a cash forecast will be provided below.

At the end of a forecast month, you can check your forecast by looking at your actual bank balance and any changes to your payables and receivables. Then create a forecast for a new month; every time a month is completed, create a new forecast. As you continue to do this, you will be able to create a reliable picture of how much your cash outflows will be so that you can make plans on how to meet them based on your estimated receivables.

However, you should not create a forecast longer than 12 months, since it becomes more difficult to make them accurate. The further you try to look into the future, the more likely it is your forecasts will be inaccurate due to the growing number of variables that will crop up that you cannot predict. For instance, your sales could go down due to factors such as economic downturns. The tax rates may also increase or the banks could increase their lending rates.

Continuously monitor your cash forecast. As you continue to update and make adjustments to your cash forecasts, they will become more accurate and give you a better idea of what your cash requirements will be in the near future. Thus, they will become an important tool in your cash management process, since they will tell you what your cash requirements will be and if you will be generating enough cash to meet them.

For instance, in three weeks you will have to make bank payments and your payroll on the same week. If you see that you will not have enough cash to meet your obligations, you can start making plans in advance as to how to manage your finances.

In addition, you can use the cash forecast to make strategic decisions for your business. For instance, if you are planning to open a new branch office, you can forecast how much it will cost for the next six months and then look at if you will have enough receivables to meet it.

As you continue to make your cash flow projections, your estimates should come closer to the actual figures. The variance should be no more than 5% more or less, but should not exceed this. The larger the variance, the less accurate your projections will be.

If you see large differences, you should examine your assumptions to determine if they are valid or if you need to change them. Look for variable expenses as well as cash inflows that could affect your cash flow. In particular, consider seasonal expenses that could affect your cash flow, such as insurance payments, increased taxes due to higher sales and higher payrolls.

Find ways to control cash flows. Businesses should start exploring ways to maximize cash flow before it encounters crisis situations. These can include:

Encouraging customers to make payments more quickly. You can offer them incentives for making early payments, such as offering discounts for instance. While this may hurt your profit margin, it can provide you with short-term cash inflow and help cash flow management.

Have stricter guidelines for approving credit, and make sure that they are strictly enforced. And make sure that receivables are collected on time. If possible, assign a staff member to monitor them and contact debtors to collect payments that are due.

Extend terms for payables. You should negotiate to get the best deal for paying your creditors. Try to extend them to sixty or ninety days. At the same time, make sure that you pay on time to avoid late fees and other penalties.

Encourage existing customers to buy more. It can take time and money to acquire new customers, so it is quicker and cheaper to maximize customers you already have. You can do this by offering incentives such as contests and deals. You can also start a referral program to get existing customers to refer your business to others.

Take medium and long-term steps to increase cash flow. Aside from these short-term steps you can explore more fundamental opportunities to increase cash flow. These can include:

Improving inventory management. Maintaining too much inventory ties up cash by converting it into non-cash assets. Thus, you have to look at your inventory levels to determine if you are managing it efficiently.

Disposing of unwanted assets. If the company has assets it can sell without compromising its operations, it can dispose of them to generate quick cash flow. Alternately, the company can sell the assets and then lease them back for a short time so they can continue to use them.

Launching new products and removing unprofitable ones. The company can assess its product line, to consider eliminating ones that may not be doing that well as well as exploring if there is a demand for ones that the company is not offering.

Reducing capital expenditures. These are funds allocated for buying, maintaining and upgrading physical assets such as equipment, property and buildings. Companies should explore ways to reduce capex such as setting limits for capitalization spending and assessing these expenses to see if they will really contribute to profitability or improve operational efficiency.

Changing pricing. This is something that a company should only consider as a last resort since it may hurt cash flow in the short-term. However, if they are offering a unique product or service, then a moderate price increase may increase cash flow in the medium to long-term.

Reducing staff. This is also a move that should only be considered as a last resort. At the same time, however, the company should be constantly assessing its staffing to identify areas of redundancy where staff can be reduced without hurting operations and employee morale.

Creating a Cash Flow Forecast

Cash flow forecasting allows you to determine what your business' cash requirements will be in the future and your ability to meet them. In addition, it allows you to identify periods when cash outflows will exceed inflows so you can plan for them.

The forecast is vital for short-term and long-term planning. In the short-term the forecast can identify months where you will need more cash than usual, such as when you will have to pay large annual expenses. In the long-term, you can identify periods when it is the best time for business moves such as expansion, which will require a lot of cash.

When preparing your assumptions for your cash flow forecast, there are four areas to look at:

Sales. Sales represent the main source of cash inflow for businesses. However, forecasting sales can be challenging, particularly for new businesses who do not yet have past sales figures to look at. The difficulty stems from the fact that there are many variables that can affect sales that may be hard to foresee, such as economic downturns or competition from another company.

If your business is already operating, you can use past sales figures as the basis for making your forecasts. It would be particularly helpful if you have one year's worth of sales, since you can identify seasonal periods when sales are particularly higher or lower.

You will have to divide sales figures into those made on a cash basis, and those sold on credit. Credit sales are considered receivables and you will have to take into account the timing of when they will be settled in your forecast. For instance, if your customers make payments using credit cards, and the payment period is thirty days, you can estimate that a bulk of your sales will come due a month after the sales were made.

Other sources of cash inflows. Aside from sales, there are likely other sources of cash coming into your business. For instance, you may expect inflows from the sale of assets and income tax refunds. You may also see capital inflows from bank loans.

Expenses. These are recurring cash outflows that are related to the operation of your business, such as employee payroll and payments for utilities and rent, as well as those related to sales such payments to suppliers.

Other cash outflows. In this category, you can include one-time expenses such as purchases of equipment and other assets, loan repayments and dividends. It also covers investments, since these also represent an outflow.

These assumptions should be realistic in order to be useful for planning. In fact, it would be better if you erred on the low end rather than the high end, since assumptions that are too optimistic may result in cash shortfalls later when the actual cash coming in is lower than what was predicted.

Now that you have assembled all your assumptions, you can create your cash flow forecast. The best way to create your forecast is by using an Excel spreadsheet. Start by creating twelve columns, which will represent months in the coming fiscal year. On the left side of the spreadsheet, use the following categories:

- Operating cash, opening. This category lists how much cash you have at the start of the month.
- Income from Sales. Create separate categories for cash and credit sales.
- Other cash inflows. List down inflows not related to sales, such as bank loans, income from other sources, etc.
- Expenses. List down all the expenses, including those made on a one-time or seasonal basis.
- Surplus/(Deficit). Subtract cash outflows from inflows. If you experience a surplus, then you have excess cash that you can put aside as a buffer or re-invest into your business. If there is a deficit, then you still have time to plan how to deal with it.

Here is a simplified cash flow projection statement that covers two months.

Internal Cash Flow Projections

October-November 20xx

	October	November
Operating Cash, opening	1,000	1,150
Income from Sales	46,000	48,000
Cash	26,000	27,000
Credit	20,000	21,000
Other Cash Inflows	7,000	5,000
Bank Loans	5,000	5,000
Other Income	2,000	--
Total Cash	<u>54,000</u>	<u>54,150</u>
Expenses		
Employee Payroll	44,000	44,000
Debt Repayment, principle		
And interest	5,000	6,000
Utilities	1,500	1,400
Rent	850	850
Insurance	500	500
Professional Fees	1,000	1,000
Purchase of Assets	--	9,000
Total Expenses	<u>52,850</u>	<u>62,750</u>
Surplus/(Deficit)	1,150	(8,600)

Assumptions:

- 75% of credit sales will be collected 30 days after sale
- 25% of credit sales will be collected 60 days after sale
- Payables are due in 15 days

Ensuring and Maintaining Profitability

Businesses exist to make a profit. If you are not making a profit, then you will not be able to meet your strategic objectives for your business, whether it is to grow it or to reach a valuation where you will be able to sell it in the future. As we have already discussed, you can determine if you are making a profit using a profit and loss statement.

However, there is more to profitability than simply making money. It is a measure of your capability to earn a profit relative to your resources. Even if a company makes a profit, it does not mean that it is profitable. Or in layman's terms, profitability measures your business' ability to make a profit.

In order to ensure that you maintain your profitability, there are three issues you have to look at:

- Your margin. Generally, margin refers to the difference between the selling price of a good or service and the cost of producing or acquiring it.
- Your mark-up. Mark-up refers to the difference between the retail cost of a product or service and its wholesale cost. It is expressed as a percentage of the cost.
- Your breakeven point. This is the point at which you are no longer losing money and you begin to see a profit.

While it may seem that margin and mark-up are interchangeable, in fact they are different since they provide you with different information. This will be further explained below.

Measuring Margin

There are generally two types of margin: gross and net.

- Gross margin refers to how much of your net sales are left after you deduct cost of goods sold. It tells you how much money you are making. However, a small amount of the gross margin is still used which pays for administrative and selling expenses as well as taxes.

- Net margin, on the other hand, subtracts these residual expenses. Thus, it is smaller than the gross margin.

Gross Margin is computed as follows:

Gross Margin (Gross Profit) = Net Sales – Cost of Goods Sold

Net sales refer to the amount in sales that you receive less commissions and discounts to customers. Once you've done this computation, you can also express Gross Margin as a percentage as follows:

Gross Margin (percent) = Gross Profit/Net Sales X 100

To illustrate how these calculations work, let's say that you have $100,000 in sales and have spent $10,000 on supplies and $30,000 on labor. Thus, your gross profit is $100,000 – ($10,000 + $30,000) = $60,000. Your gross margin (%) is $60,000/$100,000 = 0.6. This means that you keep $0.60 for each dollar of sales.

Gross margin is important because it tells you if your sales are enough to cover your costs. The higher the margin, the more quickly you will achieve break even and become profitable. If you have already been in business for some time, high gross margins will make it more likely you will have a high net income and operating profit margin.

Net margin is computed as follows:

Net Profit (Margin) = Net Sales – Gross Profit

Net Profit (%) = Net Profit/Net Sales X 100

Net margin tells you how profitable your business is overall. In addition, you can use it to compare your company's performance with others in the same industry.

Using Mark-Up to Set Selling Price

Mark-up refers to the amount of profit the company wants to earn, above the cost of producing or acquiring the product. For example, if the company spends $10 to produce Product A, and it wants a 10% markup, then the selling price is computed as follows:

Take the markup rate and subtract 1. Thus, 10% - 1 = 90 percent.

Divide the product cost by the results of the first step. Thus, $10/.09 = $11.11. Your selling price is $11.11.

You can also compute the markup for a product that already has a selling price as follows:

Markup (%) = (Sales – Cost of Goods Sold)/Cost of Goods Sold X 100

Computing the Break Even Level

Break even refers to the level at which you have covered all your costs. Past this level your business is starting to make a profit.

It is computed as follows:

Break Even (in dollars) = Expenses/(1 – Cost of Goods Sold/Net Sales)

Break Even (%) = Expenses/(Unit Selling Price – Unit Cost to Produce)

There are a number of reasons why it is important for you to know what your breakeven point is. One of the most important is that it helps you to assess what your pricing policy should be based on what your true costs are.

Business costs can be divided into two categories:

- Fixed costs are those that remain constant, such as rent payments, insurance and IT costs. They are not directly related to the process of revenue generation.
- Variable costs are those related directly to sales generation, and so are subject to change depending on factors such as volume of sales generated or services delivered and volume of production.

Once you have determined what these costs are, you can determine what your selling price should be. Keep in mind that you cannot just set the price based on what you want your profit to be, since you will still have to take into account what the market will accept. If you price your product too high, you risk hurting your sales.

You can then estimate how many units of the product you will have to sell at this price in order to meet your break-even point. Once you have reached break-even, all you need is to cover the marginal costs of producing more product in order to make profits.

Improving Your Cash Flow

Running a business requires you to have a regular supply of cash in order to meet your daily expenses as well as your current obligations, such as servicing your debt. Ensuring that you have adequate cash is also known as managing your working capital.

The cash conversion cycle refers to how long it takes, in days, for a company to convert inputs into cash. It starts with purchasing stock from a supplier, and then selling it (if it is a finished product) or processing it into a finished good for sale (also known as "work in progress"). You then sell the product and collect the cash, and then the cycle repeats again.

You may have noticed that between each stage of the working capital cycle, there is a time delay. It takes time to process the stock before it is ready for sale for instance. You obviously also have to sell the product before you can collect the cash for it. And while the cycle is going on, you still need to have cash flow to meet your business expenses.

Here is a way of computing how long it takes from the start and end of your cash conversion capital cycle, which is known as the cash conversion rate.

Cash Conversion Rate = Days Inventory + Days Receivables - Days Payable

Days Inventory measures how long it takes for a business to convert its inventory into sales income. It is computed as follows:

Days Inventory = Inventory / Cost of Sales X 365

To illustrate, if the company has a year-end inventory of $40,000 and sales for the year of $300,000, then its days inventory would be:

Days Inventory = 48.7 days

This means that the business sells its whole inventory within a nearly 49-day period.

Days Receivables refers to the length of time it takes a company to collect payments from sales. It is computed as follows:

Days Receivables = Accounts Receivable / Sales X 365

To illustrate, if the company has accounts receivable of $75,000 and sales of $300,000, their days receivable would be:

Days Receivables = 91.25 days

This means that, during the year, the business collects its receivables every 91 days

Days Payable Outstanding refers to the length of time before a business pays its payables to its creditors. It is computed as follows:

Days Payable Outstanding = Accounts Payable / Cost of Goods Sold X 365

Thus, if the business has accounts payable of $8,000 and cost of goods sold of $150,000, its days payable outstanding is:

Days Payable Outstanding = 19.5 days

This means that the business pays its bills almost 20 days after it receives them.

Thus, the Cash Conversion Rate is:

Cash Conversion Rate = 48.7 + 91.25 – 19.5 = 120.45 days

This means that from the start to end of the Cash Conversion cycle takes 120 days. Obviously, the shorter the cycle, the better since it means that the company's capital is not tied up in inventory or work in progress.

Working capital management is about ensuring that the cycle moves as quickly as possible so that you can always have a supply of available cash. Having cash on hand ensures that you won't have to rely on external sources of financing such as short-term loans or bank overdrafts, which can be costly.

Here are some of the aspects of working capital management that you need to focus on:

Stock management

Ensuring that you have the right level of stock available means that you will be able to meet your customers' needs. However, when you have too much stock, it also represents a drain on your resources, since you will have to pay for their storage and other costs such as insurance and controls to ensure their security. Maintaining stock is estimated to cost from 10% to 30% of its value.

There are three elements involved in efficient control of stock:

Stock review. This aspect involves inventorying your stock to determine just how much you have and its value. Then you have to review what items are selling the best so that you can focus on them, and order less of those products that are not selling as well. In your review, you should also keep in mind that certain products sell better during particular seasons, so you need to be aware of these trends.

It is also important that you identify stocks that are aged, as well as excess products. You will have to find a way to eliminate these from storage since they represent a drain on your resources. Your action plan can involve selling slow moving stocks and donating those that are not moving.

Finally, make sure that you have a system in place for tracking the movement of your stock. This means that your records should constantly be updated so you'll know how much stock you have at any one time, as well as what types of stocks are in the inventory. This will help to create a sensible reordering policy in which you'll only place new orders when needed.

You should conduct a physical inventory at least once a year and then match it with stock records you've kept throughout the year. The records and the physical count should match; if they don't then you need to do a physical count more often until you have identified and corrected the irregularities.

Stock purchasing policy. As you run your business, you'll notice that there are certain products that are consistent sellers for you. These are known as your "core" stock and it should be part of your purchasing policy that you never run out of them to avoid disappointing your customers and losing sales.

At the same time, you should be familiar with the volume of sales each product generates. This will help you to order the right quantities, so you'll always have stock available of the most popular products while not carrying too much of those which don't sell as well. Keep in mind that stock that is in your warehouse and not selling represents tied-up cash that could be put to better use.

You also need to be able to strike the best deals with your suppliers. But you should avoid discounts based on volume purchases, since you may end up buying too much and hurting your cash flow. Instead, try to negotiate discounts based on prompt settlement of payables or ask your supplier for more frequent but smaller deliveries.

Operational issues. With regard to the earlier issue, try to work with a supplier to schedule just in time deliveries, in which the stock is delivered only when it is needed. This allows you to spend for stock only when you need it, freeing up cash that you can use for other requirements.

You should also implement a sales policy to ensure that stock moves faster. For instance, you can put slow-moving items on sale or selling items bought at bargain rates at a lower price. The ultimate goal of your sales policy should be to turnover products as quickly as possible so they can be converted into cash.

Stock Management by the Numbers

There are also ratios that you can use to help tell you how well you are managing your stock.

The Days Stock ratio will tell you how frequently you are changing your stock.

Days Stock = Stock on Hand / Cost of Goods Sold X 365

For instance:

Stock on Hand = $4,310
Cost of Goods Sold = $41,300

Days stock = 38.1 days

Thus, on average, stock is held for 38 days before it is turned over

The days inventory ratio tells you how often you are turning over your stock per year.

Days Inventory = Cost of Goods Sold / Stock on Hand

For instance using the same figures:

Days Inventory = 9.6 times

This means that, on average, stock is turned over 9.6 times in a year. If the rate is too low, then you risk having an inventory of aged stock. If the rate is too high, then you may not have enough stock on hand, then you may not have enough to meet your customer's needs.

How can you most effectively use these ratios? Compare your ratios with industry averages. You should also look at how your ratios are doing over time, since this will tell you how effective your stock management policy is.

Managing Your Supplier Payments

Payments to suppliers are one of your biggest expenses, and will have a substantial impact on your cash flow. Generally, when your business is starting out, suppliers will require you to pay in cash upon delivery since you don't yet have a history with them. Once you have been working with them for some time and you already have a relationship with them, they will be more likely to allow you to acquire stock on credit. This will free up cash flow since you can pay your suppliers later once you have sold the stock.

There are three factors to consider in managing your supplier payments:

Choosing the suppliers you work with. The first step in choosing suppliers is deciding what they provide that is most important to your business. Among the factors to consider are the quality of the products they offer, the terms they provide, their prices and their returns policy. List down which of these are most important to you.

Next, make a list of suppliers you think you would like to work with based on the considerations on your list. Then undertake a check of the credit and trade references of each supplier. You can then create a shortlist from which you will make your final choice based on their trustworthiness as well as what they have to offer you.

Once you have chosen one or more main suppliers, make sure that you also have a backup or alternative supplier so that there won't be any disruptions in your stock acquisition. In addition, you should periodically check how your suppliers are performing. It is worth keeping in mind that your priorities may change and the supplier you are using may not meet them, so you should consider looking for a new one.

Supplier's Payment Terms. Once you have chosen a supplier, you can negotiate payment terms with them. Keep in mind that the two of you are negotiating for different things – you want longer terms while the supplier wants shorter ones. Remember that payment should start from when there is full delivery of stock unless you have agreed otherwise with the supplier. Aside from the terms, you can consider if it is worth it to accept early payment discounts or if these would hurt your cash flow.

You also have to create a system for dealing with damaged or unusable goods, since this is a perennial issue. If there is a problem with deliveries, make sure that you communicate this to the supplier at once. Never withhold payments for unsuitable or damaged goods until you have spoken with your supplier.

Make sure that you pay your suppliers promptly – not late and not too early. Create a schedule for when payments will be sent, such as once monthly at the end of the month. Once you have established this schedule, stick to it unless there are circumstances that will cause a delay. If so, inform your supplier promptly and tell them when the payment will be made.

Review the terms regularly and look for alternative suppliers who may be willing to give you better terms. However, discuss these terms with your existing suppliers to see if they are able to match them before you switch.

Maintaining supplier relationships. In order to ensure that you maintain good relationships with your suppliers, meet with them regularly to discuss how things are going. They may be willing to help your business by providing improved terms or tell you about new products you may be interested in.

In addition, create a system for your suppliers to communicate with you in case there are problems such as non-receipt of payments and delayed payments. For instance, you can assign a staff member who will act as the point person for communicating with the supplier.

Supplier Payment Ratios

Here are some useful ratios that can help you better manage your payments to suppliers.

The creditor days ratio will tell you how often you pay your suppliers every year. If you are consistently paying late, you may be damaging your relationship with your suppliers. On the other hand, if you are paying early, you may be hurting your cash flow.

Creditors Days = Accounts Payable / Stock on Hand X 365

To illustrate:

Accounts Payable = $3,210
Stock on Hand = $41,000

Creditors Days = 28.6 days

Compare this figure with your payment terms to determine if you are managing your supplier payments well.

Managing Pending Orders

Once you have accepted an order from a customer, you have to process it. You have to create efficient systems for managing these orders since the quicker they can be finished, the sooner you can bill the customer and receive the cash payment.

Here is a sample of the process used to realize pending orders. You can use this as the basis for creating your own procedures or compare it with one already in place to possibly identify improvements.

Record the order when received. Make sure that all the relevant details are recorded, such as when the order is due, what the payment terms are (i.e. if payments for partial delivery will be invoiced) and if there are any additional costs that will be incurred. If there are specific materials that will have to be custom-ordered, ask the customer for an up-front deposit before you accept the order.

In addition, before you accept orders, make sure that you have enough stock on hand to meet them. Avoid orders where you have insufficient stock unless you are confident it will be delivered promptly. Keep in mind that delays in processing may not only cost you money but also hurt your relationship with your customer.

Track orders of work in progress. There should be procedures in place to track outstanding orders based on priority. In addition, potential or actual delays should be highlighted so that steps can be taken to deal with them.

Invoice upon delivery. Once the order is delivered to the customer, send along an invoice.

Keep records. You should keep track of when orders are to be completed and delivered, and the invoice date. This will help you to predict your cash flow so that you can better manage it.

In addition, you should regularly review your order fulfillment process to identify bottlenecks and other areas for improvement.

Dealing with Debtor Collections

Since your business relies on a regular flow of income from your customers, it is important that you put systems in place to ensure efficient and timely collections are made. These systems will not only ensure that you are paid on time, they can also avoid unnecessary and stressful effort.

There are three elements to consider in efficient collections from customers:

Controlling credit. If you are planning to extend credit to your customers, make sure that you do a thorough check to see if they are creditworthy. There should be a system in place to do this.

Once you have vetted the customers to whom you will give credit, rank them in order of the credit risk they represent. You can use this list to determine what credit limits you will give to them.

There should be systems in place to monitor credit usage. Once a customer has exceeded his limit, there should be a procedure for dealing with it, such as sending them a notification. The customer should not be allowed to make another order before the matter has been resolved.

In addition, you should also be checking your customers' credit status on a regular basis. Keep in mind that this can change based on economic conditions and their personal circumstances.

Establishing payment terms. Once you have decided on your payment terms, these should be clearly indicated on the invoice. The staff should also be familiar with these terms and stick to them without exceptions.

There should be systems in place to ensure that these payment terms are followed. It should include a procedure for dealing with late payments, such as ensuring that reminders are sent promptly and follow-ups are made. There should also be a procedure for dealing with returns that includes prompt credits to customers.

Managing customer relationships. Establish procedures for communicating regularly with your customers, particularly key ones that are important to your business. If possible, arrange to visit their premises since this will give you insight into their business requirements and how you can meet them.

In addition, you should review your customers' payment history. If you find a customer is consistently late in making payments, reach out to them so you can discuss the matter. You can also choose to give incentives to customers who pay early.

There should be a system in place to deal with orders that are not fulfilled as expected, which includes procedures on how to deal with payments. If an order will be delayed, communicate promptly with the customer. Tell them when the order will be met or discuss alternatives on how to fulfill the order.

Using the Receivables Turnover Ratio

This ratio will tell you how efficiently you are collecting your accounts receivable, or the amounts owed to you by your customers and other debtors. Accounts receivable have to be collected on time to ensure regular liquidity; otherwise your cash flow may be severely affected. This ratio is generally computed every year, although it may also be calculated on a monthly or quarterly basis.

Receivables Turnover = Accounts Receivable / Net Sales X 365

To illustrate:

Accounts Receivable = $16,000
Net Sales = $42,000

Receivables Turnover = 139 days

This means that, over the past year, the business collected accounts receivable every 139 days.

The best way to use the receivables turnover ratio is to track it over time, that is, compute the ratio for several years and look at the progression. By doing this, you can detect patterns or trends that indicate the company's collections policy might need to be changed.

In addition, there are a number of other factors that need to be considered that affect the receivables turnover:

- Credit policy. A high receivables turnover might indicate that the company is extending credit to customers who are late payers or unable to pay.

- Statement of accounts errors. If the accounting department is issuing invoices with errors that need to be corrected, this can increase the length of time before receivables are collected.

- Discounts for early payments. A short receivables turnover might be the result of the company offering early payment discounts. In this case, it should be worth considering if the increased cash flow is worth the cost of the discounts.

Efficiency of collections staff. If there is not enough staff working on accounts receivable or if they do not have the training or the tools to do their job efficiently, this can affect collections and increase receivables turnover.

.

5 BUDGETING AND THE FUTURE OF YOUR BUSINESS

Budgeting is something that everybody is, or should be, familiar with. Essentially, you budget when you take what you earn in a particular pay period and allocate it in such a way that you won't spend more than what you're earning. For a business, however, budgeting involves looking into the future and projecting income and expenses.

Why do you need to prepare a budget? There are a variety of reasons, which include:

- Knowing how much you have to earn to meet your expenses. By projecting what you will spend in the next year, you will also know how much revenue you have to generate to meet them.

- You can determine how much you can pay yourself. By knowing how much your expenses will be over the coming year and what your estimated sales are, you can determine what salary you can pay yourself.

- You will need a budget if you plan to get a business loan or are fundraising. The lender will ask to see your budget for at least the next three years since this will help him determine if you are a good credit risk. The budget will show your capability to repay the loan based on your projected cash flow.

- Your budget can help identify if you have extra cash. If you have excess capital that will not be used for operations, you can include provisions in the budget for how to invest it. For instance, you can place it into money market accounts or make longer-term investments such as buying the property on which the business premises are located.

Creating a Profit and Loss Budget

This financial statement is one of the most valuable tools you will need to ensure that your business is profitable. Although it is prepared in the same way as a profit and loss statement, it uses estimated data of future transactions to estimate future income and expenses. They are used as a way for managers to determine the business's profitability over the medium-term as well as what its financial requirements will be.

There are two ways of preparing a P&L budget:

- Incremental. This method uses financial activities from a previous period as the basis for the budget.
- Zero-based. This method does not take past periods into account when preparing the budget.

The secret to ensuring that this statement will be useful to you is determining that the assumptions used to prepare it are as realistic as possible. One way to do this is to look over past data and use this as the basis for estimating future data. It would also help if you look over financial information from your industry to see if your assumptions are in line with them.

To illustrate how to make assumptions, here is an example:

Sales
Forecast – will grow by sixty percent in the next year
Based on – forward orders placed by customers
Risk – sales may decrease or stay constant

Cost of Goods
Forecast – will stay constant at fifty percent of sales
Based on – current contracts with suppliers
Risk – increase in stock prices

Payroll
Forecast – will increase by twenty percent next year
Based on – industry standards
Risk – cash flow problems

Here is a sample of what should be in a profit and loss budget

Sales Revenue
Other Income

Interest

Investment

Others

TOTAL INCOME

EXPENSES

Fixed Expenses

Rent

Phone (landline & cellphones)

Internet

Office Supplies

Advertising

Professional Fees

Insurance

Employee Salaries/Benefits

Loan Repayments

Miscellaneous Expenses

Variable Expenses

Raw Materials

Cost of Production

Wholesale Price of Goods

Packaging and Shipping

TOTAL EXPENSES

NET PROFIT BEFORE TAX

It should be noted that some fixed expenses might become semi-variable expenses depending on the volume of your business. For instance, during holiday seasons when there is greater demand, you may hire temporary workers and this will increase your payroll expenses. You may also need to make short-term loans and this will increase your loan repayments later on.

If you prepare your budget on a monthly basis, you can create a column for the actual figures so you can compare how accurate your assumptions are.

Tips for Getting the Most Out of Your Budget

Have the right mindset when preparing your budget. Keep in mind you are not supposed to account for every dollar spent. Instead, the budget should be a tool and guide for you so that you can make more informed and better business decisions.

Now that you have identified where your sources of income are coming from, you can start looking ways to improve your revenues. For instance, you can reduce your expenses by looking for alternative suppliers or buying supplies in bulk.

You can also use the budget to identify areas where you may need to make adjustments. For instance, if your rent accounts for 25% of your total expenses, it may be time to find ways to reduce it.

If you have extra cash, you can use your budget to identify the best areas in which to use it. For example, you may want to pay off any high-income debt in order to save on interest in the medium-term. Or you may notice that you need to invest in a particular piece of equipment that will make your business more efficient and thus, more profitable.

The budget can identify risks that you will need to prepare for. For instance, you may need to create a plan for risks such as if you suddenly lose a major customer or if business is disrupted due to a fire or other unexpected disaster.

Prepare a budget as often as possible. Although it is okay for larger businesses to make a yearly budget, you may need to prepare it on a quarterly or monthly basis. This will not only ensure the budget is more accurate, it will also help you to prepare for contingencies since small businesses have less resources to be able to cover them.

KPIs and Forecasting Your Financial Future

A business can also generate its own indicators for budgeting, in order to measure its financial performance and set business goals. These are known as key performance indicators or KPIs, which are defined as measurable measures that a company uses to determine how effectively it is meeting its strategic and operational goals. KPIs set targets that you can ensure are met by managing your budget.

KPIs have four essential characteristics:

- Directional – they must help determine if the company is improving its performance
- Actionable – they must lead to practical actions that can lead the company to effect necessary changes
- Quantitative – they can be presented as numerical data
- Practical – they can be integrated with the business' current processes

One simple way to determine what qualifies as a KPI is to ask the question: if this indicator moved either upward or downward significantly, would it affect the business in a meaningful way?

Why use KPIs? Here are four reasons:

Allows the company to measure its goals. KPIs have two parts – a metric and a target. The metric is the numerical measure – such as the percentage by which the company is exceeding its budget for shipping costs – that the business is tracking. The target is the objective that the business is trying to meet, such as keeping increases in shipping costs to no more than 10 percent annually.

Helps the business manage its spending. As shown in the target above, KPIs can help the company to keep its expenses to within a certain goal. For instance, if the spending on shipping exceeds the 10% goal, the company can start looking for ways to reduce or control it.

Keeps your employees accountable. KPIs provide your staff members with quantifiable targets that they know they'll have to meet. They also give supervisors a yardstick by which they can measure employees' performance and give them guidance as to which areas they need to improve.

While this may seem like yet another burden for employees, in fact it can help boost morale. When the KPIs provide small targets over the short-term that can be easily met, employees can enjoy the psychic rewards of being given positive reports for achieving their goals.

Make forecasts more accurate. If you create a KPI using financial information from a past period, you can create future forecasts based on how accurately the business has met the KPI's target.

Here are some tips for developing KPIs:

Focus on a small but effective group of KPIs. One of the greatest temptations when using KPIs is using too many in an attempt to measure everything. Start by identifying the most important areas to focus on and then create KPIs for them.

The KPI should lead you to positive actions. The indicator should highlight areas where you might need to take corrective action. For instance, a KPI that measures your return on investment (ROI) for particular marketing campaigns can highlight which ones are successful. This can help you decide which ones to keep and which to discard or change.

Create KPIs that measure the experience your customer is having. You can get data on these by conducting customer surveys. Examples of these KPIs include:

- Net Promoter Score – This measures how many customers are recommending your business to others.
- Sales/Marketing Conversion Rate – This KPI measures how likely a customer is to take a particular action such as making a purchase.
- Satisfaction rate – This indicator measures how happy a customer is with your service.
- Resolved customer issues – Look over the complaints that your customer service team have received to see how many of them have been resolved to the customer's satisfaction.

Use KPIs that are based on your business' stage of growth. If you are just launching your business, for instance, you can use KPIs such as customer acquisition and customer awareness of your products. If you are expanding your business, you can look at rate of customer growth, cost per customer acquisition and average order size.

Look at both lagging and leading indicators. Lagging KPIs measure something that has already happened, while leading KPIs look at something that will happen in the future. Examples of leading KPIs are penetration in new markets and brand recognition.

While most companies focus on lagging indicators, it is also important to look at leading ones. Think of them as a way of driving your business in the direction in which you want it to go. They also allow you to identify future trends as well as help you determine if you are on track to achieve your goals and how close you are.

6 GETTING THE MOST FROM VENDORS THROUGH PROPER MANAGEMENT

Every business works with vendors, which are people or organizations that supply them with goods and services. Each of these vendors has their own contract and payment terms, which have to be carefully managed in order to ensure a smooth working relationship with them. For instance, you don't want to delay payments for goods delivered, or for the vendor to not be able to speak with a person about an unresolved issue.

Although most people see vendor management as being only about managing your relationship with them, it actually covers a wide range of activities. The process actually starts with researching vendors by getting in touch with them and asking for quotes. These quotes not only include pricing but also turnaround times and capabilities.

Once you have decided which vendors to work with, you have to negotiate contracts with them. After you start working with them, you have to evaluate their performance and then provide them with feedback. You also have to arrange a payment schedule and ensure that it is met. If you cannot pay your vendors for whatever reason, you have to get in touch with them promptly and tell them when payment will be made.

As you can see, the vendor management process can be complicated and requires a lot of time and resources, as well as people skills. Here are the four steps of vendor management:

First, establish the business goals you want vendors to meet. Ask yourself, what do you want and expect from your vendors? The answer to this question will help you to choose which vendors to use and how to manage them later.

Second, select the vendors. Now that you have set your criteria, you can start assessing candidates. This step is crucial to the success of your business so you should take the time to ensure that you choose which vendors will best meet your needs.

Third, manage your vendors. This is the day-to-day process of working with your suppliers, ensuring that they perform according to contract terms and providing regular feedback. You may need to assign a staff member to act as a dedicated vendor manager to work directly with them and handle the relationship.

Fourth, ensuring that the vendor consistently meets the performance objectives you have set for them. This is where the vendor manager plays a vital role as he communicates regularly with the suppliers to influence their performance.

When it comes to building a relationship with your vendors, here are four important things to keep I mind:

Always communicate your priorities to them. A good vendor understands that your priorities have to be theirs as well, in order to ensure the success of the relationship. This is why you always have to share relevant information with them such as launch dates for new products and services. Communicate with them as often as possible and ensure transparency in your dealings with them.

Work with your vendors on business strategy. Your vendors are also partners and collaborators on your business, and have a vested interest in your success. So you might want to work with them more directly, i.e. by inviting them to participate in meetings that involve products they are suppliers for. They may be able to provide invaluable insights that could make the product more competitive by improving it or making it cheaper. At the very least, you should always be in touch with them via phone or communication methods.

Build long-term relationships with them. When your vendor knows that you are building a long-standing relationship with them, they are more likely to be invested in working with you. This can also lead to more cost-savings in the long run for your business as your vendor is more likely to provide you with preferential treatment and discounts. They may also provide you with suggestions as to how to reduce costs.

Focus on agreements that are mutually beneficial to both parties. There are some managers who think that strong-arming their vendors during negotiations will provide them with better terms. But this will only build resentment and make it less likely that you will build a lasting relationship with them. Instead, negotiate in good faith and seek to find agreements that will benefit both parties.

Things to avoid when dealing with your vendors include:

- Making changes to payment and contract terms unilaterally without consulting with them
- Making emergency orders at the last minute
- Changing orders frequently after they have already been made
- Delaying the handling of inbound deliveries

Remember to treat your vendors with consideration and respect in order to get the best out of them. Avoid the "customer is always right" mentality that makes you treat vendors poorly just because you can.

How to Choose Vendors?

When it comes to vendor selection, it is very important that you decide in advance what you want from them. For instance, you can set criteria such as:

- Capacity to meet orders. How large are the orders you anticipate when ordering at peak?
- Minimum orders. What is the smallest quantity the vendor will allow you to order from them?
- Delivery methods. What specific methods does the vendor use?
- Returns policy. What are the conditions the vendor sets for returning damaged or unusable goods? What after-sales support do they provide?

- Payment terms. What conditions does the vendor set for payments? Are they willing to extend credit and under what terms?

- Lead times. How long will it take between the time you place and order and when it will be fulfilled?

- Storage and handling. Where does the vendor keep their product?

Once you've set your criteria, you have to find potential vendors who will meet them. You can do so either by publishing your requirements in trade publications and request bids or approaching vendors you are interested in directly and asking if they are interested in providing estimates and proposals.

Make sure that the quotes you request include full details such as what products you need and the quantities required, quality standards, lead times and delivery details. In addition, you can ask for details about their financial health, the stability of their suppliers as well as why you should consider using them.

Once the bids are in, you can evaluate them using your criteria and create a shortlist of candidates. You can ask those you are seriously interested in to visit your offices separately to hold discussions about how they can meet your requirements. Weed out those who don't meet your criteria.

If you still have a number of candidates and have not yet made a final decision, you might want to ask those still in the running to come in for a final round of talks. At this stage, you can provide them with more specific details as to what you need so that they can sell themselves more thoroughly.

Keeping Vendors Accountable

One way that you can ensure the performance of your vendors is to establish a system of penalties and incentives. This will ensure that the supplier will be rewarded for meeting their performance targets, but will also be punished if he fails to achieve them. Having both penalties and incentives is essential to ensuring that your suppliers stay on track.

Penalties and incentives should be included in any service contract with the vendor. They should also be mentioned in purchase orders and, if applicable, letters of credit. The performance indicators that trigger incentives and penalties should be clearly defined and lines of communication should always be open to avoid potential threats.

However, you might not want to apply incentive and penalty clauses to all your vendors, since this may overwhelm your vendor manager. Instead, you should focus on the ones that are most critical to your business. Doing this allows you to focus on those vendors whose performance represents the highest risk to your organization.

For other vendors, you might want to use alternatives such as establishing a rating system that you can use to assess performance and provide feedback to suppliers. You can also create an approved list of vendors that you will work with, and exclude suppliers who don't live up to your requirements.

You can also continuously evaluate your vendors at every stage of the procurement process. This will help to forestall any problems before they become more serious.

How to Evaluate Vendor Performance?

There are a wide variety of methods that you can use to evaluate the performance of your vendors. For instance, you can ask your employees to fill out evaluation forms or complete surveys asking them to assess the vendor's performance. You can conduct periodic vendor audits where you ask representatives of the company to meet at a certain location so that you can talk to them about their performance.

But no matter which method you use, it is important that you establish a set of guidelines or metrics that you will use for evaluation. These can include:

Percentage of orders received. This metric measures how many orders you made were actually fulfilled by the vendor. You can generate data using purchase orders and receipts, and the measurements are usually done on a monthly basis. However, you should exclude orders in which the supplier notified you in advance that they would be unable to meet, although you may also want to take this into account if it happens often.

For example, you can use this formula:

Supplier Performance = Quantity Received/Quantity in Purchase Orders X 100

Thus:

Purchase orders (January) 300,000
Quantity Received (January) 295,890
Supplier Performance = 98.63%

On-Time Delivery. This metric measures what percentage of deliveries is received based on the agreed-upon schedule. You can use baselines such as the arrival time promised, when the delivery is booked-in to the warehouse or even a window (such as between 5:00 and 7:00) during which the delivery should be received.

Here is an example of how this metric could be measured:

Inbound Deliveries Checked-in at Arrival Time/Total Inbound Deliveries X 100

Thus:

Inbound Deliveries Received On-time = 7 crates
Total Inbound Deliveries = 9 crates
Supplier Performance = 77.78%

This means that 77.8% of the supplier's deliveries were received on-time.

Other metrics you can consider include:

Financial health. Measuring this metric can be challenging but would be worth it for key suppliers. A supplier who suddenly declares bankruptcy or suffer financial problems can disrupt your supply chain. You can ask the company to provide you with financial data and then analyze it using financial ratios that we've already discussed. To get a better overview of how the company is doing, you can compare these ratios with industry standards or those of their competitors.

Customer base. If your vendor relies mainly on your company for their business, it may be a cause for concern since they may not be financially healthy. One rule of thumb that many big box retailers use is if your business represents 30% of the vendor's revenue base.

Quality metrics. These metrics refer to the condition the product was in when it was received. For example, was the shipment received in a neat-looking package with no dents? Was the shipment delivered without any errors? One metric you can use is what percentage of shipments was in good condition when they were received.

Vendor Cost Management

One of the major concerns for startups and small businesses is managing their costs. One way that you can lower costs is by negotiating with your vendor for lower prices. Of course, these negotiations have the potential to be contentious, particularly if you already have a signed contract with the vendor. Here are some strategies to help you get the best costs from your vendor.

Make sure that you are always professional when dealing with your vendor. When you tell them that you need to lower costs, they will understandably be angry. Just explain what problems your business is facing and why you need better pricing from them.

Make sure that the vendor also gets something in return for their concession. For instance, you can extend the current contract with them.

Don't focus on getting the lowest possible price from a vendor. Keep in mind that if the price goes too low that it becomes unprofitable for the vendor, they will have to cut costs elsewhere. This might compromise the quality of the service you get from them, which will also impact costs in the long run.

When negotiating with a vendor, tell them what your target price is. By being upfront with the vendor about what your expectations as for price as well as quality, he can decide if he is able to meet your price,

If the vendor is initially uncooperative, keep in mind that you have leverage. Remember that you have the option not to renew your contract with them. This might help convince the vendor that it is in their best interest to renegotiate in exchange for a renewal.

It might also help with negotiations if you mention that they have competition. But make sure that you don't disclose confidential information such as pricing. The vendor might be more willing to compromise if they know that a rival is in a good position with you to make a deal.

Keep in mind that there are other ways to save costs rather than by lowering prices. For instance, you can negotiate more advantageous payment terms, such as extending the repayment period or giving you discounts for early payments.

Consider a vendor consolidation strategy. If you are dealing with several vendors to source your requirements, look into the possibility that you can reduce the number of vendors to a select few and ship more from them. If you increase your volume orders from a particular vendor, they may be able to reduce prices and lower shipping costs.

Vendor consolidation also reduces your cost structure by reducing the number of locations from which materials are shipped. It also saves time and effort since you have to deal with a smaller number of vendors and reduce the number of billings you have to pay.

Negotiate supply agreements with your vendor. Another way you can cut costs is by reducing or eliminating your inventory costs of ownership. The holding costs of storing parts and other supplies in a warehouse until you are ready to use them can add up, particularly if you are keeping them for extended periods. In addition, there is the risk that these will become damaged and unusable.

You can pass on this risk to the vendor by negotiating a supply contract with him. Essentially, this means that the vendor will hold the supplies for you and bear the holding costs. At the same time, you should realize that the vendor will not hold these indefinitely since they also have holding expenses, so you will have to periodically renew the contract.

Make sure that any negotiations you undertake with a vendor will end with an agreement that is mutually beneficial to both parties. Remember that your vendor is ultimately one of your business partners and thus, has a vested interest in your success. If you have to make concessions, keep in mind that these can be beneficial in the long run even if it seems you are giving something up in the short-term.

Also, negotiations should always be done in good faith. Never lie to your vendor since this they may find out eventually and this will sour your relationship with them. Negotiation does not mean that you have to be totally honest and reveal everything, but if you have to disclose something, always tell the truth.

7 FUNDRAISING – WHICH OPTION IS BEST FOR YOU?

When you are running your business, at some point you will need additional capital to meet operating costs during rough times or to finance its expansion and growth. Unless you are willing to continue funding your business with your own money, you will have to start looking for ways to raise the capital that you need. There are a number of ways you can access financing, and finding the right one can spell the difference between success and failure for your business.

Businesses can access financing through:

Debt. This is sourced from external sources such as banks and other lending organizations. Examples of debt include:

- Bank loans
- Overdrafts
- Shareholder loans
- Commercial bills

- Advances

Equity. This consists of investment made by the owner or other sources in exchange for a share of the business:

- Owner's capital
- Partnership equity
- Stock share issuance

Internal funds. This comes from cash generated by the business through sales and other sources. Examples include:

- Retained earnings
- Sales of assets
- Reduction of working capital

Debt Financing

Should you avail of debt to finance your business? There are a number of advantages to using this finance option over equity:

- You get to retain ownership of your business. The lender does not have the right to tell you how to run your business, nor is he entitled to a share of your profits. Your only obligation is to make your loan payments on time.
- Your debt payments are tax deductible. Generally, business loans are considered a business expense and thus, you can deduct them

from your income. However, this is dependent on the tax laws of your country.

- It is easier to budget debt payments. Since you know how much you will have to pay in interest and principal, you can easily account for them in your budget for the upcoming months.

Of course, there are also disadvantages such as:

- You have to make your debt payments no matter what. Even if your business is not doing well or you have a slow month, you still have to service your debt. This may mean personal sacrifices such as taking a smaller salary.
- You have to make sure that you have sufficient cash flow to repay the loan. As we already mentioned, there may be unforeseen circumstances that can affect your cash flow. This may force you to take moves to cut costs in order to free up cash such as reducing staff and selling assets.
- You will have to put up a collateral. This is an asset that the lender can claim if you default on the loan. Most lenders require collateral of some sort to protect their interests.

What are your options for debt financing? Below we will describe some of the most common sources, each of which has its pros and cons. However, their availability may differ from country to country.

Term loans. These are basic loans that require you to make repayments on a fixed schedule over a certain period of time, and at a fixed interest rate. Businesses generally use them to purchase supplies and equipment for operations. The lender accepts property as collateral for the loan, which allows him to offer more affordable terms.

Line of credit. This is a flexible form of financing that allows you to draw on capital when you need it, in order to meet your business needs. It provides you with flexibility since you only access cash when you need it rather than giving you money in a lump sum.

The line of credit helps with your cash flow since you can repay the money you have accessed once your business income comes in. It also allows you to manage your lending costs since you only pay for money that you actually use.

Equipment financing. This is a loan taken out to buy equipment for your business. This can be used for virtually any piece of equipment, ranging from vehicles to computers. The equipment itself is the collateral for the loan, which makes approval easier. The loan is paid through monthly installments, which usually come with fixed interest rates.

However, since you will have to take interest charges into account, the cost of buying the equipment through financing may be more expensive than if you bought it outright. In addition, the lender may require you to make a down payment or make advance payments before approving the loan.

Merchant cash advance. Here the lender gives you a lump sum, trading it for a share of future sales. The provider automatically debits a certain percentage of your sales or other revenue to repay the loan. Instead of being charged interest, the amount you will repay is computed by multiplying the loan amount by a 'factor rate', i.e. 1.3.

The main advantage of these cash advances is they are very easy to get. You can be approved even if you have bad credit, and you can get your cash in as little as 24 hours. You also don't need to provide collateral since your future revenue acts as security for the loan.

However, there is no fixed repayment rate, since the payments are based on a percentage of your sales. Thus, if your sales revenue declines, repayments will also fall, meaning that it will take longer to repay the loan. Cash advances are also more expensive in the long run since the total amount to be repaid is less than if you were able to get a term loan with the average interest rates.

Small business loans. These are loans are designed specifically for small business owners and that are provided by sources such as online lenders, credit unions and banks. Depending on the country where you live, there are government agencies that have programs that help you get approved for these loans and may also partially guarantee them.

However, it can be difficult to be approved for these loans. You will have to provide extensive documentation to explain what the loan will be used for. You may also be asked questions about your previous experience running a business if you're seeking a loan for a startup company. Thus, it would increase your chances of being approved for a loan if you have a business plan. We will discuss how to make a business plan in a later section.

When should you avail of debt financing? One important thing to remember is that you will have to start repaying the loan shortly after you have received the money. Thus, you have to consider if you will have the cash flow to make debt payments. Take the following into consideration:

Will the financing be used for fixed or variable expenses? If you are using the loan to buy equipment, then you have to make repayments from your business income since fixed assets will not generate cash returns. On the other hand, if you are using it for business costs such as buying materials, you should make sure that it would generate cash inflow.

Am I just starting out? Unless you qualify for a start-up small business loan, you would be better off using your own money or finding funding from friends or family. Your business will probably be losing money at the beginning, thus making it unlikely that you will be able to make loan repayments.

Can I rely on timely payments of receivables? If you are assured of having a steady cash flow from your customers, then getting a loan may be for you since you will be able to make your payments.

When deciding which option to take, consider the following:

How much financing do you need? Getting a ballpark figure will help you decide on the best option. You also have to take into account if you have the means to repay the loan.

What purpose will the loan be used for? This will help you decide which loan option is best for you. However, there is a more important consideration to keep in mind.

What type of loan can I qualify for? Ideally, you should be able to pick the type of loan that best suits your requirements. But in reality, you are limited in your choices by which options you qualify for. The factors that lenders take into account may include your credit score, your business' annual revenues and how much money you have in the bank.

What type of business do you have? If you have a seasonal business, you may have trouble getting debt financing since you don't have consistent sales volumes from month to month. This means that you may have difficulty making regular debt payments. You may need to look for an option that does not require you to make set payments, such as a line of credit.

Writing a Business Plan

Of course, you will need a business plan to secure funding, but there are a lot of other reasons why you should write one.

A plan can help you plan the future of your business. For instance, you can detail future scenarios that can affect your business so that you can make contingency plans to deal with them. You can also write down what your goals are for your business so that you can determine what is needed to meet them.

A plan can justify to lenders and investors why they should put money in your business. A business plan gives you the opportunity to implicitly promote your business. For instance, you can promote what makes your business unique and what would make people want to buy from you.

A plan will help you manage your cash flow. When you make a business plan, you have to justify where your income will be coming from as well as what your expenses will be. For instance, what percentage of your sales will be made on a credit basis, and when will they be paid? What expenses do you have to meet and when do you have to meet them? By knowing this information, you can determine how much funding you will need for your business requirements.

A plan will help you to attract talent. A business plan represents what your concrete vision is for your business. It is something that you can show to people you are interested in recruiting so that they will know what your business is about and why they should join it.

A plan will help you create an exit strategy. At some point, you may decide that you want to sell your business after it has become successful. A business plan can help you decide the best option for liquidating your business, such as passing it on to another individual, taking it public through an IPO or selling it to another company.

There are a variety of ways that you can write a business plan. Below we will present the traditional format used that includes all the essential sections that the plan should have. However, you don't need to include all of these in your plan, since you can pick which of these are most appropriate for your business.

Executive Summary. Although this section is presented first, you may choose to write it last, after you've finished with the other sections. The executive summary provides a brief overview of your business, including what products and/or services it offers and basic information about it, such as where the offices are located, how many employees you have and who your management team is. It should be no more than two pages long.

Description of the Business. In this section, you will provide a detailed description of your business. It should answer the following questions:

- What industry is your business located in? What is the current outlook of the industry and what growth opportunities do you foresee in the future?

- What are your company's strengths? What makes your company competitive in its industry? What are the factors that will help your company to succeed?

- What are your personal strengths? What can you bring to the business that will help it to succeed?

- What is the main audience for your business? Who will you market it to?

- What is type of legal ownership of your business? Is it a sole proprietorship, a partnership or an LLC? Why did you choose this ownership type?

In addition, the description should include your mission statement. The statement should answer the following questions: What is your business about and what is the philosophy behind it? What are your products and services? What are your goals for your business?

It should be just a few sentences long and be succinct so that a person who is reading it can get an understanding of your business at once. While there is no recommended length, you should aim for around 30 to 50 words, but no more than 100.

Marketing Plan. In this section, you will describe how you will market your business. Start by describing any market research you have performed to determine that there is a demand for your products or services. What type of research have you performed? The two types of research are: primary (by generating your own data) or secondary (by accessing published sources such as studies, trade publications and census data).

Analysis of the Competition. In this section, you will detail who your major competitors are, as well as what their strengths and weaknesses are. Then, you will enumerate what strategies you will use to become competitive.

If you want to create a more detailed analysis, you can create a table comparing your company with those of your main competitors. Start by detailing what products or services you offer compared with those of your rivals. Then you can create comparisons in other categories such as the quality of the products, their reliability, their price, the reputation of the company, credit policies and the method for marketing the business.

Design and Development. This section of the business plan discusses your main product or product line. It should cover three main areas:

- Product development. Describe the design of your product and how it was developed.
- Market development. How will you market your product?
- Organizational development. What are the financial and human resources you need to meet your production and marketing goals?

This section should also include a Development Budget, in which you will list the costs required to design, produce and market the product, including:

- Staffing requirements
- Materials
- Marketing costs
- Overhead
- Administrative costs
- Sales & marketing costs

Operations and Management. In this section, you will describe how your business will be run on a day-to-day basis. Aspects of operations you may want to include:

- Details of your suppliers – who they are, what they provide your business, their delivery and credit policies and how reliable they are.
- The legal environment – what are the regulations that affect your business, what licenses and permits you need, what insurance you need and if you have any patents or trademarks (existing, purchased or pending).
- Production details – how do you make your products? What inventory and quality controls do you use? What products do you have in development?
- Staffing. How many employees do you have? How are they organized? What are the different departments you business has and what are their functions? How do you recruit new staff members?
- Location. Where do you plan to set up your business? What are its physical requirements (building type, amount of space required, utility needs)? How much will it cost (rent, maintenance,

remodeling) to set up the business there? Will there be any construction requirements and how much will they cost?

Financial Plan. In this section you will include financial statements that will give an idea of how your company will do financially, including:

- Three-year sales forecast. This statement will estimate what your sales will be for the next three years. The first year should be broken down into months, while the second and third years should have projections on a quarterly or yearly basis. It should be broken down into the following categories: total units sold, price per unit, sales income (unit sales X price), unit costs and cost of sales (unit costs X units). Then calculate gross margin by subtracting sales income less cost of sales.

- Expenses budget. Project how much you will spend to run your business. Create separate categories for fixed costs such as payroll and rent and variable costs such as costs of production and advertising expenses.

- Cash flow statement. Bring together data from the first two statements to get an idea of how much cash is going into and out of your business. Don't forget to take into account credit sales, which will not be paid at once, so that you'll know how much cash you can actually expect in order to meet your expenses. It should also be broken down into a month-to-month basis for the first year.

- Profit and loss statement. This statement will show how profitable your business will be by subtracting the gross margin by total expenses.

- Balance sheet. This statement will show the projected net worth of your business. You can start by estimating what fixed assets your business has, then estimate other assets such as your accounts receivable and inventory. Then estimate your liabilities starting with any business loans you have taken out and your accounts payable.

- Breakeven analysis. In this section, you will project when your business will start to break even (sales = expenses), after which it should start to become profitable (revenue exceeds expenses).

As an alternative to the traditional business plan, you can write a "lean" business plan. This plan contains only the most essential elements to explain your business. It is ideal for startups who have a relatively simple business model or you need to generate a plan quickly to show investors or lenders. There are also many formats for this type of business plan, but here are some of the important elements to include:

Business strategy. There are three elements you should include: what is your business about, what your products and services are and who your target audience is.

Business tactics. This section includes specifics on finances, products and marketing. Marketing tactics should include information on how you plan to promote your business and reach your target audience (online and offline methods). Product tactics include what your product or service lines are, delivery options, apps for ordering the product and the company website. Financial tactics covers the financing methods the business avails of.

Assumptions, Metrics and Milestones. In this section you will enumerate the performance metrics you use to measure the success or failure of your business, such as sales targets and expenses, as well as tailored kpis such as sales per employee, conversion rates and web traffic. Next, name some of the performance milestones that you should hit, such as when you expect to launch the product, when you expect to reach breakeven and when you will become profitable.

Financial Forecasts. In this section you will do basic forecasts of financial metrics such as sales, costs, expenses and cash flow. You don't need to present tables, just give yearly figures in a bullet point format. You should also include the assumptions you used in the projections, such as a 90% collection rate on accounts receivable.

You can also use the Business Model Canvas template, which is one of the oldest lean business plan formats. It has nine components:

Value Proposition. What is the unique value that your product/company brings to the market?

Key Activities. How will your business gain a competitive advantage over others in the market? Highlight things like the way you sell your product or how you use technology to reach customers.

Key Resources. What are your most important assets? These could include staff, intellectual property or capital.

Key Partnerships. Who are the other companies your business will work with? These include suppliers and subcontractors.

Customer Segments. Who is your target market? Try to be as specific as possible so you'll get an idea as to who your customers are.

Customer Relationships. How will your business interact with your customers? What is the customer experience that you plan to give them?

Channels. What are the methods you will use to communicate and interact with your customers?

Revenue Structure. How will you make money? For instance, will you sell online or offline? List all of your revenue streams.

Cost Structure. Will you focus on maximizing value or reducing costs? Define what your strategy will be and what the associated costs are.

Whatever format you choose, you should always periodically review and update your business plan. Remember that businesses are not static and conditions are always changing, and your business plan should reflect these changes.

Equity Financing

This is the other main financing alternative for those seeking capital for their startup businesses. Basically, it involves asking individuals and organizations to invest in your business in exchange for ownership shares. This also entitles them to a share of the profits from your business.

The main advantages of equity financing are:

- You are not required to make monthly payments. This frees cash flow that you can use for operations and to expand your business.

- The investor may be able to provide you with valuable advice. Your investor may have either invested in other businesses before or started their own business. Thus, they are in a position to advise you and help you avoid many of the common business mistakes you might make.

- You can have access to large amounts of funding. If you have a good business idea that investors believe will be profitable, they will be willing to provide you with big amounts of capital.

The disadvantages include:

- It can be difficult to quality for equity financing. Most investors will only put money in ventures that they believe have a high potential to be profitable in the near term. Keep in mind that one out of every two small businesses fail within their first five years of operation.
- You might lose control over your business. Since your investors have ownership stakes in your business, they might feel they have the right to step in and interfere with the way it is run. This is why you have to ensure that you see eye-to-eye with the investor as to what your business is about and how you will run it.
- You will dilute any profits you earn from the business. As we already mentioned, investors effectively become co-owners of the business, and thus are entitled to share in the profits. This means less profits for you in the long-term.

What are the types of equity financing that are available for small businesses?

Money from friends and family. This is usually the option many small startups take when they have no other options for financing. The main advantage of this option is that these investors may not ask for ownership shares but simply expect that their money will be repaid. The disadvantage is that, of course, there is a risk that you may lose their money if your business fails.

"Angel" investors. This term refers to wealthy investors who are looking for businesses that can provide them with a high return on investment. However, this also means that they have high standards for the businesses they will put their money in. They usually have limited participation in the business since they are investing due to their belief in the abilities of the entrepreneur running the business.

Venture capital. These are professional investors whose participation may require that you give them a say in the running of your business, i.e. by giving them a seat on your Board of Directors. And, of course, they are looking for businesses that will give them high rates of return.

Mezzanine financing. This type of financing is a hybrid of debt and equity. The investor extends a loan to the business and the company pays it back when it can. If the company fails, the investor has the right to convert the loan to an ownership share. This protects the investor since they can still recover their investment if the business goes bankrupt.

Royalty financing. This type of financing is tied to the success of a particular product. The investor makes money ("royalties") by taking a share of its sales when the product is finally brought to market.

Government programs. Depending on the country where you live, there may be government programs that help small businesses find funding. As with small business loans, the agency itself does not provide funding but brings businesses and investors together.

How do you find equity investment?

If you are looking for angel investors, try angel investment networks that bring together investors who are interested in a particular niche or entrepreneur networks. If you know any financial advisers, you can also ask them for recommendations.

One thing to remember is that when you pitch your business to angel investors, their standards are lower. They don't necessarily need to see a business plan, but if you can sell your business, and yourself, successfully to them, they will invest in you.

You can find venture capital companies by looking for networks or associations of venture capitalists in your country. Keep in mind that when you approach a venture capital investor, you will have to provide a lot of documentation to convince them that you have concrete ideas and strategies about how to run and grow your business. If you've already been running your business for some time, you will need to present them with financial statements showing them how it is doing.

In recent years, many small businesses have sought financing through crowdfunding platforms. You pitch your business on these platforms and you set a funding goal. Users of these sites then kick in certain amounts in exchange for perks, which may include early access to the product or service, discounts when it is launched or personalized thanks for very small investors.

There are two general types of crowdfunding:

Reward/Donation. This is the type of crowdfunding offered on platforms such as IndieGoGo or Kickstarter. Investors donate money that you will use as capital to launch a venture, such as creating a product. In exchange, they get perks such as a prototype of the product or the right to buy it early before it is brought to market.

Securities. You can avail of this type of crowdfunding on platforms like Wefunder or StartEngine. This is more like the traditional type of financing in that investors also expect that they will have a share in the venture. Thus, you will have to prepare the same type of documentation as if you were pitching to a professional investor, and upload it to the platform. You can then promote your crowdfunding proposal even outside of the platform, such as through social media or through marketing campaigns.

Internal Sources of Financing

This type of funding is not suitable for all businesses, but if you can manage it, you can enjoy many advantages. Internal financing refers to capital raised within the business itself rather than from outside sources. These include:

Owner's Investment. The people behind the business provide startup capital or additional capital needed by the business. The majority of businesses need capital to continue operating until they achieve profitability, otherwise they would fail.

Retained earnings. If a business is fortunate enough to be profitable, then it can use retained earnings to finance its operations. Retained earnings refer to net profits (gross profits less expenses) that are not distributed by the company to shareholders as dividends.

Sale of assets. If a business has fixed assets that it does not need for operations, it can dispose of them to raise cash. If these assets no longer have book value because they are fully depreciated, the business can even enjoy a taxable gain if it sells them.

If the enterprise is fortunate enough to be located on real estate whose value has appreciated beyond that of the business, then it can earn capital by selling the property and relocating to a more affordable location.

Receivables collection. The company may find that it has a lot of collectibles that it is not collecting or is not being paid on a timely basis. Thus, it may be able to raise capital by increasing its collection efforts.

The benefits of using internal funding methods are similar to those of availing of debt in that it does not dilute your ownership in your business, as well as being able to maintain control over it. But in addition, your company will be more attractive to investors or potential buyers since it is not carrying a lot of debt.

Bootstrapping Your Business

If you have little access to external sources of financing and you don't have a lot of capital, you can still start and run a small business through bootstrapping. Bootstrapping is a term that refers to starting your business with limited capital and without seeking other sources of financing.

The basic principle behind bootstrapping is that you can actually fund a business with very little capital. There is a prevalent belief that you will need at least $500,000 to fund your business. But studies have shown that more than 80% of successful small businesses are actually self-funded using substantially lower capital – sometimes for as little as $10,000.

How can you bootstrap your small business? Here are some tips to help you get started:

Choose a business model that generates money quickly. This will ensure that your business is generating cash flow so that you won't burn through your available capital. For example, you can encourage customers to buy your product via a recurring monthly subscription by offering deep discounts vs. one-time sales.

Create a separate bank account for your business. Since you are self-funding your business, you have to ensure that you exercise strict control over your capital. Having a dedicated account for your business allows you to keep track of your spending as well as your cash inflow.

Run your business from home. Instead of setting up operations in a separate office, you can set up operations at home. If you have other team members, you can work with them remotely through Skype and other online communication methods.

Negotiate terms with distributors and suppliers. For instance, you can save money by arranging to dropship your products rather than maintaining an inventory. If you are running a service-based business, you can generate some cash flow to cover your costs by asking customers for a certain percentage of the fee as a retainer.

Take on a partner. Working with a partner can be beneficial to small startups since they can not only share the costs of the business but also bring their own particular skillsets to the enterprise. Of course, you should make sure that you will work well with any person that you plan to partner with, i.e. that you will complement each other.

Don't hire people to do jobs you can do yourself. Since money is at a premium, you don't want to incur additional expenses by outsourcing jobs. Take a look at what needs to be done for your business and consider which tasks you can do.

In addition, if there is something you don't know how to do, consider learning it. Alternately, there may be available software that can help you do certain things, such as bookkeeping or doing your taxes. Even if you have to pay a fee for these applications, it will still cost less than if you had to hire a bookkeeper or accountant.

Live a thrifty life. When you choose to bootstrap, you should accept that the majority of your money will go towards running and growing your business. So you will have to live a very frugal life and cut down on many expenses. You may even have to downsize your lifestyle, i.e. move to a smaller apartment or take on a roommate to share rent and other expenses.

Be persistent. As a micro-business that is just starting out, you will probably have trouble getting suppliers to work with you. This means that you will have to work double-time to build connections with them and convince them to take a chance on you. Doing this may even require that you share your life story with them.

Don't scrimp on incorporation and getting your website domain. There are certain business expenses that you will have to spend money on, since not doing so will cost you more in the long run. For instance, you will have to be sure that your business is incorporated properly. Avoid using online incorporation services since these may cause problems for your business.

Ensuring that you get your desired website domain is also essential. A URL that reflects the name of your business will make it easier for your customers to find you. In addition, you should not think that you can delay getting your domain until your business is generating more income, since once you have started to become successful, it may become more expensive.

Consider what revenue opportunities you will pursue. As a struggling business, it can be tempting to chase opportunities that promise a big revenue bump. However, you should take the long view and consider if these will align with your vision for your business or if they will be a distraction. Always keep in mind that what you want is to grow your business and you should only pursue revenue opportunities that contribute to this goal.

Create a business budget. Look at what it will cost to run your business, as well as what you anticipate your earnings will be. Then create a business budget that reflects your estimate cash inflow and outflow. You can use this budget as a way to reduce your business costs by ensuring that you control your expenses.

Become a paperless business. One of the hidden costs of running a business is the cost of printing bills and invoices. While these expenses may seem minimal in the short-term, they can add up in the long run. Transition to a digital bill payment and invoice system, and send out paper billings and invoices only upon request. You can even charge customers a small fee for printed billings as a way to defer your costs.

In addition, you can start keeping your files on your computer rather than maintaining these on paper. Of course, you should make sure that you keep backups online, such as on cloud storage, as well as on a physical medium such as a flash drive.

Look for cost-effective ways to market your business. These days, there are many ways that you can reach your customers without having to spend a lot of money. For instance, you can market through social media such as Twitter or Facebook.

You can also start a blog for your business. There are many advantages to having a blog. You can position yourself as an authority in your particular business niche. It is also a way to address your customers' common concerns. And you can optimize your blog posts using keywords and other search engine optimization techniques so that it can help drive traffic to your site.

Microtest your product. Before you launch, you can test the viability of your product through "microtesting", which means developing a version of your product or service with limited features so that you can test how viable it is online. Examples of how you can do this is by offering the product on a mockup website to see how many visitors click on the link. You can also try taking a few sample products and offering them on eBay to sell how salable they are before you commit to launching them in earnest.

Look for small business grants. Although applying for these grants can be a time-consuming process, it is worth it if you qualify. Look for grants from private groups and state agencies, and do your research thoroughly so you'll know what exactly is involved.

8 RISK MANAGEMENT FOR SMALL BUSINESSES

Risk is something that every business has to face. Fortunately the harm that risks can do to your business can be minimized with a risk management plan. In a business context, risk refers to the possibility of loss arising from various factors. Risk management involves identifying and analyzing the various risks confronting a business and finding a way to avoid them. If the risk is unavoidable, risk management involves finding a way to mitigate them.

Types of Risks

Risks can be classified into two distinct types. Internal risks are those that a company faces due to its operations. On the other hand, external risks are the ones that arise from economic events outside of the company.

Examples of internal risks include:

Human risks. These risks arise from the company's human resources. Possible human risks are:

- Low employee morale. If your employees are unhappy, it can have a negative impact on your business. For instance, demoralized employees might be neglectful at work, or even outright negligent, which can hurt your operations.

- Fraud and theft. Employee fraud and theft is a constant risk that businesses face, no matter how carefully they want to create an honest working environment. For instance, employees may steal office supplies or use timecard fraud to work shorter hours than they are actually being paid for.

- Death and illness. If an employee of a company, or even the owner, falls ill or dies, it can disrupt a company's daily operations or even pose a risk of the company closing.

- Poor vendor performance. This risk involves suppliers failing to live up to what was agreed upon in their contracts, such as delays in delivering or sending products that have to be sent back due to quality issues. This can cause delays in shipping to customers and damage the company's reputation.

- Strikes. If employees go on strike for whatever reason, it can disrupt operations and hurt a company's cash flow.

Technological risks. These are risks that arise from equipment or other technology that a company uses in its operations. For example, older vehicles used by the business may break down or operate less efficiently, causing delays in delivery. On the other hand, newer equipment may require employees to navigate a learning curve for its use, meaning that it cannot be integrated into a company's operations at once.

Information technology also poses technological risks. Software that is not updated may stop working properly and affect your office operations. Older computers may suddenly crash or slow down, delaying office work.

Physical risks. These are risks to the physical assets of the company, such as:

- Building risks. The most common risks faced by a company's physical plant include fires and explosions.
- Hazardous materials risk. Companies often use potentially toxic materials in their production processes, such as poisonous gases, fumes and acid. These materials present a workplace risk to workers if they are accidentally exposed to them.

Financial risks. These are risks related to a company's cash flow. An example of a financial risk is carrying a lot of short-term debt, since this may hurt your cash flow if the lender suddenly calls it in. if you extend too much credit, this is also a financial risk since if customers delay payment or you are unable to collect your receivables, your cash flow will be hampered and you may not have enough capital to fund your operations.

Operational risks. These are risks that arise from a failure in the company processes that disrupts its operations. For instance, if your business has a server failure, it may affect the normal running of the office since it cannot access vital files. An employee may also make a mistake that causes the company a lot of money, i.e. accidentally debiting too much from your company account.

Strategic risks. These risks stem from the failure of your company's business strategy to deal with changing market conditions, and thus the company becomes unprofitable or fails to meet its business goals. For instance, if you fail to anticipate that your product will eventually become obsolete and nobody wants to buy it anymore, this is a strategic risk.

Reputational risk. This risk stems from damage to a company's reputation, which can erode your customers' trust in your business and make them no longer want to buy from you. Examples of reputational risks include lawsuits against the company, product recalls and other types of negative publicity.

Reputational risk may actually be either an internal or external risk, depending on what causes the damage to a company's reputation. For example, there may be negative publicity due to an allegation from an external source against the company. Product recalls may be the result of negligence on the part of staff tasked to do quality control, or the failure of those assigned to product development to anticipate flaws.

Examples of external risks include:

Market and economic risks. These are risks caused by changes in market conditions that can impact a company's revenues and its profitability. These include:

- Market changes. These risks happen when conditions in the market change, causing either an increase in production costs or a decline in demand for the company's products or services. For instance, there may be a recession that causes people to buy less of your product.

- Competition. These risks happen when a company becomes uncompetitive due to various factors. For instance, a competitor may introduce a product that sells better than yours or reduces the price of an existing product so that it is cheaper.

- Policy changes. These risks arise from changes in the fiscal or economic policy of the government. For instance, the central bank may raise lending rates, making the cost of borrowing more expensive. The government may reduce tariffs on imported products that are directly competitive with your products.

Natural disasters. These are risks to your business caused by hurricanes, earthquakes and other "acts of god". An earthquake can cause damage to your physical plant, disrupting production or affecting your normal operations.

Compliance risks. If a government agency makes changes in regulations that your company has to follow, it can disrupt your operations while you become compliant. This can reduce sales and hurt your profitability. But introducing new products can also result in compliance risk, since you will have to consider if they meet regulatory requirements.

A company can also face compliance risks if they export products or have operations outside their home country. You have to consider if your product is compliant with the rules of the country you are exporting to, because otherwise they may not let them in.

Creating a Risk Management Plan

The one important thing to remember about a risk management plan is that it does not mean that you will eliminate risk altogether. Rather, it helps you to identify which risks you cannot avoid so that you can create measures to mitigate their effect on your business.

The first step is to identify what risks your business faces. For internal risks, you can do this exercise on your own or consult with staff and other shareholders.

One method you can use to identify internal risks is to perform a SWOT analysis of your business. SWOT stands for Strengths, Weaknesses, Opportunities and Threats. This analysis helps identify internal and external threats to your business.

Start by taking a sheet of paper and dividing it into four quadrants. Label each with one of the SWOT categories.

Strengths. The main thing to consider is what makes you and your business stand out, and what attributes you have that will allow you to meet your goals. Use the following guide questions:

- What do you have to offer your business?
- What unique skills do you have?
- What specialized knowledge do you possess?
- What experience do you have that can benefit your business?
- What do you do better than other businesses in your niche?

Weaknesses. What attributes do you and your business have that could prevent you from succeeding? Use these guide questions to help you:

- What additional resources do you need?

- What additional skills do you need or experience to meet your goals?

- What areas of your business do you need to improve upon?

- In what areas do you think you are wasting time and/or money?

Opportunities. These last two quadrants consider external factors that could affect your business. Opportunities refers to external factors that you can take advantage of which could benefit your business. Guide questions to consider include:

- Are there new customers that you can target?

- Are there new technologies that you can take advantage of to improve your business?

- Are there new products and services that you can expand into to grow your business?

Threats. This quadrant looks at external factors that could hurt your business. Guide questions to consider include:

- What are the strengths of your largest competitors?

- What is happening in the economy that could hurt your business?

- What is happening in the larger industry where your business is located?

- What obstacles does your business face?

- What are your competitors doing that may be making them more competitive?

To identify external risks, you can conduct a PEST analysis. PEST stands for Political, Economic, Socio-Cultural and Technological. These are the different categories of changes in the business environment that can affect your company.

Here are some guide questions to help you identify political risks:

- When are the next elections, and how could their outcome affect local and national policy?
- Which candidates are most likely to win and what are their policy positions?
- Are the rule of law and property rights fully fleshed out in your country? How widespread is corruption? How likely are these to change in the short- and medium-term?
- Are there upcoming legislation or changes in taxation and fiscal regulations that may have an effect on your business?
- Are there any pending changes to business regulation that can impact your business?
- Is the current policy environment moving towards deregulation or more regulation?
- What is the government approach to issues such as environmental protection, consumer rights legislation and corporate policy and social responsibility? How will these impact your business?
- Are there any other political factors that might change in the short- and medium-term?

Here are guide questions for economic factors:

- What are current economic conditions? Is the economy growing, shrinking or stagnating?
- Are disposable incomes on the rise or dropping? Would this change in the short and medium-term?
- Are key exchange rates stable or fluctuating?
- How is access to credit for businesses and individuals? How will credit conditions affect your business?
- What are employment and unemployment figures like? Will there be a pool of skilled labor you can draw from and what will labor costs be like?
- How is the local economy reacting to globalization?
- Are there other relevant economic risks that you have to consider?

Here are guide questions for socio-cultural factors:

- What are the levels of social, education, and health mobility like in your country? Are these undergoing a transformation and what will the impact be on your business?
- What are the religious beliefs prevalent in the general population?
- What lifestyle choices are people making?
- What are the trends in the job market and employment patterns that you notice?
- What are people's attitudes towards work?
- What are the current social views and taboos prevalent in your country? Are these changing?
- Are there any other socio-cultural factors that can affect your business?

Keep in mind that many of these socio-cultural factors differ among different demographic groups, i.e. various age groups and genders.

Here are guide questions for technological factors:

- Are there emerging technologies that could help make your business more efficient and productive?
- Are your rivals using any new technologies that could make them more competitive?
- How has technology affected working patterns, i.e. the Internet and new communications technologies has made working from home practical.
- In which areas are government and private groups doing the most research? Are they developing any upcoming technologies that could affect your business?
- Does your country have technological hubs that your company could work with?
- Are there any other technological factors that can affect your business?

You can also consider using other analytical tools such as:

STEEPLE – Socio/Demographic, Technological, Environmental, Economic, Political, Legal, Ethical

SLEPT – Socio-cultural, Legal, Economic, Political, Technological

PESTLE – Political, Environmental, Socio-cultural, Technological, Legal, Economic

Once you have identified potential risks, go through the list and analyze them based on the following factors:

Event: What exactly could happen under this risk?
Probability: What are the chances that the event will actually happen?
Impact: What effect will the event have on your business if it happens?
Contingency: How can you reduce the effect the event will have on your business if it happens?

Determine an appropriate response to each risk. There are five general categories of response you can have:

- *Mitigate the risk.* Take steps to reduce the probability the event will happen.
- *Accept the risk.* If the event is something that you cannot avoid, make plans to reduce its effects on your business.
- *Avoid the risk.* If you think the costs of the risks are too high, avoid it altogether. For example, you can scrap a planned product launch.
- *Transfer the risk.* You can take out insurance that will pay out in case the event happens.
- *Exploit the risk.* In the rare cases that the risk also represents an opportunity, you can take advantage of it to advance your company goals.

Warning Signs of Potential Risks

Risks do not suddenly appear out of nowhere. Usually there are certain signs that can alert you that a risk is about to emerge. Here are some of the most common warning signs that indicate risk:

Excessive reliance on a small number of vendors and customers. This represents a serious risk because your business may be in trouble if you lose even one of your customers. Similarly, if you only use a handful of vendors with no alternates or backups, you risk losing customers if even one of those vendors fails to deliver.

Too much debt. As we have already discussed, carrying too much debt is a major risk factor for businesses because it makes them vulnerable to experiencing financial difficulties. If you were to suddenly experience cash flow problems, i.e. if you generated fewer sales, then having too much debt might cause your business to become bankrupt.

To determine if you're carrying too much debt, you can look at it in relation to your owner's equity by computing the debt-to-equity ratio. Take your total debt, both long- and short-term and divide it by your equity. Generally, your debt should be no more than 50% of your equity, but you should also look at the average debt-to-equity ratio of companies in your industry to determine if you are within the industry average.

Excessive employee turnover. Generally, it is to be expected that you will experience some employee turnover. However, when the rate of employees leaving seems too high, it may be a sign that there is a deeper underlying problem with your business that needs to be addressed.

Accounting irregularities. You should conduct periodic audits of your books to identify irregularities that may indicate that there is fraud or theft going on.

Things to look out for include:

- Do the time cards match the payroll that has been submitted?
- Are there cash disbursements that you have not authorized?
- Is there too much cash going out in relation to cash inflow?
- Are there invoices that have not been reported in the system?
- Are there invoices made out to suppliers or vendors you do not recognize?

Managing Risks

Once you have identified risks, you should create ways to deal with them. Here are some examples of risk management methods you can implement for common risks.

Equipment failure. For small businesses, the failure of a vital piece of equipment can be costly since it can disrupt normal operations and cost money. The simplest way to deal with equipment failure is to have a service plan in place with the manufacturer or a third-party company. The plan should include parts replacement as well as service charges to control costs as well as ensure that any downtime is minimized.

Vendor failure. If you rely on only one vendor or a small number of vendors, your business is vulnerable in case one of them should failure to deliver. You can manage this risk by:

- Having a backup list of alternate vendors that you can source from
- Buy from multiple vendors so that you can maintain relationships with them

- Investigate your vendors to see which ones have risk factors that could cause them to fail

Information technology risks. These days, IT systems are vulnerable to risks from malicious hackers. Fortunately, there are a number of simple measures you can take to reduce these risks:

- Make people aware of the importance of online security. For instance, make sure that your employees regularly change their passwords and do not share them with anybody else, including their colleagues.

- Create tiers of access. You should limit access to the system based on the employee's job description. For instance, people who work in handling orders should not have the same access as bookkeepers or other employees who prepare financial statements.

- Invest in firewalls and other online security software. You should not rely on freeware but use paid software since this will provide you with better security. All employees should be familiarized with how to use the software to scan for viruses and its other security features.

- Conduct surprise IT audits, in addition to scheduled ones. This will help keep people aware of the importance of maintaining online security as well as preventing them from becoming complaisant.

- Uncover fraudulent transactions by using trial transactions. This will help uncover irregularities that could indicate that there is fraud going on.

Threats from competition. Just because you have a popular product or service does not mean that you should just sit back and be complaisant. There are always other companies who will look at what you are doing and think that they can do it better.

Thus, you should always be aware of competition so that you can react to it. Here are some guide questions to ask when assessing competition:

- How are the prices of competing products in relation to your pricing? Are they higher or lower?

- Are you still competitive in the market or are you losing market share?

- Is it time to revisit your pricing policy in order to remain competitive?

- Is the quality of competing products similar to or better than yours?

Employee management. Having trusted employees working for your business and maintaining a positive working environment is essential to your success. Here are some guide questions to help you assess how you are treating your employees:

- What benefits do your employees receive and how do they measure up compared with what your competitors offer? If your benefits package is not competitive, you may not be able to attract good employees.

- Is your compensation package competitive compared with what other companies in your market offer? If you want to have the best employees, you have to be willing to pay them what they're worth. Alternately, if you can't afford to pay them a good salary, give them a share of your profits.

- Are you experiencing a high rate of employee turnover? This may be an indicator that there is something wrong with your employee management policy.

- Do you provide your employees with regular training to ensure that their skills are up-to-date with what is required to keep your business competitive?

- Do you conduct periodic performance evaluations? Make sure you treat these evaluations as a way to identify ways for your employees to improve their performance rather than using it as a way to call them out for their shortcomings.

- Do you make your employees feel that you are present? If employees feel that you are an absent employer who is always out of the office, they may misbehave or simply not be motivated to do their best.

- Do you make people feel rewarded for their performance? You don't have to provide monetary rewards but what is important is that you make employees feel that they are appreciated when they perform well.

- Do you make people feel that their voices are heard? You should provide mechanisms to allow your employees not only to make suggestions but also air concerns without feeling threatened.

- Do you make sure that your employees have a good work-life balance? You should make sure that employees are not only given a regular work schedule but also provide them with time off.

Fraud. The potential for theft among employees who are charged in your organization to handle money is something that you should always be aware of. You can reduce this risk by putting in place a secure cash control system with checks at every stage. For instance:

- Whenever money is coming in, it should be logged in by two persons, with one counting it in the presence of the other.

- You should establish a hierarchy in your cash control system. For instance, if a customer asks to void a charge, it should be approved first by a supervisor.

- Create an audit trail so you can trace the inflow and outflow of money in your organization. For instance, there should be a record whenever cash is received, when money is deposited in the bank, and so on.

- Conduct periodic audits. In order to catch fraud and mistakes in recording, surprise audits should be held. During these audits, financial records should be reconciled to ensure that all the money going in and out is accounted for. If audits are held on a regular basis, there may be time for dishonest employees to hide their tracks by putting back money that they've taken or change records to conceal theft.

Managing Risk Through Insurance

Ask most people about insurance and they would say that it is an unnecessary expense. However, those people who have been in an accident and had their costs shouldered by an insurance policy would tell you that you're wrong. For small business owners, insurance is particularly important since unexpected events may affect the running of your business at best and cause it to go bankrupt at worst.

What are the different types of insurance that a small business should have?

Property insurance. This type of insurance will protect you against losses in case something happens to your business property, whether it is fire, vandalism or a natural disaster. If your insurance provider offers it, you may also consider adding loss of earning/business interruption coverage that will compensate you in case your business cannot operate.

Auto insurance. Depending on the country in which you live, this type of insurance may already be mandatory for all vehicles. However, you should make sure that you are buying enough coverage to protect you in case of accidents or other incidents that make you unable to use them. In addition, if your employees are using their personal vehicles for work purposes, you should also make sure these are covered by non-owned auto liability in case they get into an accident.

General liability insurance. This is another type of insurance that may be mandatory in many countries. Liability insurance protects your employees and your business against property damage or bodily injury caused by a third party.

Worker's compensation. This type of insurance covers employees who are hurt or even die while working, providing medical benefits and wage replacement. In turn, the employee or his survivors have to give up their right to press legal charges for damages.

Professional indemnity insurance. This type of insurance protects your business in case you are sued for issues ranging from not delivering on a commitment to providing poor advice and not meeting a quota.

Business owner's policy. This type of policy bundles together several types of coverage that a small business owner may need, including vehicle coverage, property coverage, business interruption coverage and liability insurance. You can save money because BOP coverage costs more than buying these types of coverage individually. However, you should also consider if the coverage you are provided under the BOP is enough to ensure that you are adequately protected in case you have to make a claim.

Here are some tips to ensure that you buy the insurance that you need and are adequately protected:

Consider what types of insurance your business needs. In order to avoid paying for coverage you may not need, you should assess what your requirements are. Consider the following guide questions:

- What are the mandatory types of coverage you need to have under the law?

- What is the value of your property? This will help you decide how much property coverage you need.

- Are there specialized types of coverage that are important for your particular business? For example, if you operate a restaurant, you need to have business interruption coverage since every day you are closed costs you money.

Compare quotes to find the best deal. These days, it is very easy to find quotes from insurance providers on various sites. Take the time to make these comparisons in order to find the best deal for your business.

Consider partnering with an insurance agent. An insurance agent will not only help you find the right coverage, but also work with you so that you are compliant with the mandatory insurance requirements in your country.

Make sure that you periodically review your insurance coverage as your business grows. The insurance policy you have bought in the past may not be enough to protect your business as it is now.

Keep all the documents related to your insurance. Keep complete records of the premiums you've paid and any claims you've made. This will not only enable you to protect yourself in case any problems with your policy crops up, you may also be able to use it to negotiate for lower rates.

Look for ways to save money on your insurance. For instance, for minor types of coverage, you may be able to get discounts by bundling two or more of them together and buying them from a single provider. The provider may also lower your premiums if you take steps to reduce risks, since this will reduce the chances that you will make a claim.

Creating a Business Continuity Plan

What happens to your business if operations are disrupted by an unforeseen event such as a natural disaster or a fire in your physical plant? This is where business continuity planning comes in. it enables you to ensure that your company will continue working during emergencies or, at worst, any operations downtime will be minimized.

The benefits of business continuity planning include:

The continuity of operations is ensured while downtime is minimized. Imagine how much money your business could lose if it were closed for just one day.

Now imagine that your business was closed for longer than that. Could you survive if your business were closed for a week?

It's not just short-term monetary losses that you have to think about but the longer-term impact on your business as well. How many customers would you lose if your business were unable to deliver products and services to them?

It reassures employees. Your workers are also concerned about what would happen to their livelihood in case your business is forced to close, even for a short time. But having a business continuity plan in place gives them peace of mind that their jobs are safe even when the unforeseen happens.

It helps you keep your customers. If a disaster strikes your business, your customers are more likely to stay with you if they know you have a plan in place for keeping your operations going. Even if you have to close down for a short time, you can at least give them a general idea of when operations will go back to normal.

It reassures your vendors. Vendors will be more likely to deal with you if they know that your business has a continuity plan in place. A business continuity plan reassures them that they will not lose your patronage since you will be able to continue running your operations even after unforeseen disasters.

It ensures that your supply chain will be secured. Since your vendors will more likely stick with you if they know you have a contingency plan in place, you won't have to seek new ones to recreate your supply chain after business disruptions have happened.

It helps create a culture of risk management and disaster preparedness. By involving employees in your disaster recovery efforts, you are building a culture in which everybody has a part to play in getting things back to normal as soon as possible.

Now we will discuss the process of business continuity planning.

The first step is to create a team that is tasked with disaster preparedness planning. The team should be composed of employees representing all departments in your business.

Their first task will be to identify the different disaster scenarios that your business faces which could result in disruption of operations. Aside from the natural disasters that could affect your business based on where you are located, you can also consider the following scenarios:

- Damage to the company's physical premises due to fire, natural disasters and other unforeseen event.
- Interruption of the supply chain due to various reasons ranging from vendor failure to transportation issues that prevent shipments from reaching your premises.
- Breakdown of machinery and equipment.
- Utility outrage, i.e. loss of power or water.
- Disruption of information technology systems, including loss of Internet connection, disruption of data and voice communications, and breakdown of hardware such as servers and computers.

- Loss of vital employees, i.e. due to absenteeism caused by natural disasters.

Once you've identified these scenarios, consider the impact they could have on your business. These could include:

- Delayed or lost sales or income
- Increased business expenses as a result of the event, i.e. repair costs, increased overtime, having to outsource various functions
- Customer defection or dissatisfaction
- Penalties due to failure to meet contractual commitments
- Delay of business expansion plans, resulting in loss of potential profit opportunities

In addition to identifying the source of the disruption, you should also consider how they would be affected by its duration and timing. For instance, when your network systems are down for just a few minutes, it would only be a nuisance, but if the downtime lasted for the entire day, it would have a significant effect on your business. In addition, if you were preparing an important order, it might result in a substantial financial loss.

Another thing to consider is the maximum tolerable period of disruption, or the maximum time the business can't operate before losses become unacceptable, as well as the maximum acceptable work recovery time.

The next step is to create recovery strategies for restoring your business functions. Keep in mind that in the short-term, your objective should be to ensure that essential functions are restored as soon as possible. These are functions that would have a serious impact on your business if they were disrupted for a certain period and may even lead to its closing down. Essential functions may also be those that would compromise the safety of yourself and your employees, as well as violating regulatory requirements if they were not performed.

Although each business will have its own particular set of essential functions that it has to maintain, generally there are four vital areas that you need to consider:

- Manufacturing and production
- IT systems
- Work areas
- Data and vital records

List recovery options for each of these four areas. For instance:

- Work areas. Identify temporary work areas. Create a recovery plan for ensuring that work areas are restored to normal as soon as possible.
- Manufacturing and production. Assess damage and consider how long it would take to repair damaged equipment. Consider the feasibility of leasing equipment until company equipment is repaired.
- IT systems. Consider having an IT service team on call to respond in case of problems.

- Data and vital records. Consider digitizing vital records and storing them in the cloud or on an off-site server. Identify vital paper records and make copies for off-site storage.

Then, consider which of these options is available to the company. There are generally three options:

- Pre-acquired. These options are immediately available to the company since they have already been installed in case of emergency

- Pre-arranged. The company has already made arrangements for these options to become available in case of emergencies. All that has to be done is to contact the supplier to send the option.

- Acquire. The option is not readily available and the company has to contact a vendor after the emergency has occurred to acquire it.

The final step is assessing the viability of recovery options based on expected availability time. How long will it take before the option becomes available to the company? Compare this with the maximum tolerable disruption time. Those that fall within this period are considered viable.

Here are some other metrics you should use to assess the various recovery options. You can assign each of these metrics a numerical value or a rating such as High, Low and Medium.

- Effort. How much is needed to implement the option?
- Quality. How good is the option?
- Security. How well does the option satisfy security requirements?

- Safety. How well does the option satisfy safety requirements?
- Control. How much control does the company have over the option's implementation and use?

Other tips for choosing recovery options include:

- If your office is located in an area that is prone to a certain type of natural disaster, make sure that off-site storage is located at a site that is far enough away that it would not be affected by the same disaster
- Make sure that replacement systems are identical or compatible with existing systems that you are using
- Replacement systems, whether pre-established or pre-arranged, should be tested to ensure that they will work when needed
- If you establish an off-site facility as an alternate manufacturing or other facility, it should adhere to the same environmental and safety features as your main facility
- Your off-site storage facility for your vital records should have adequate security and have proper procedures in place for maintaining them
- For flexibility, consider sourcing a mobile work area as your temporary office
- Save money by temporarily using a commercial "hot site" to recover vital systems before transferring to a "cold site" until a new permanent site or the original site is available
- When choosing vendors for your storage facilities, make sure that they have been in business for a long time

- Your backup data network and voice systems should have sufficient capacity to meet your requirements for recovery

However, the company should also look at the financial cost of the option. For instance, if you have an option that is available as both pre-arranged and pre-established, you have to consider which one is more financially viable for the company. For instance, pre-establishing an option might cost more up-front, but you have to balance this against the how long it would take the pre-arranged option to be shipped to your offices and the downtime involved.

Now that you have created your business continuity plan, it is time for you to start planning how to implement it. Create a financial analysis that considers both the impact to your business of the disaster and the costs of recovery. The factors to consider include:

- How much income will be lost if your business closes?
- What are the expenses that will still need to be met during the disruption?
- How much will recovery cost?

Compute all these costs to determine how much you should put aside for business continuity efforts. To ensure that you have enough, you should set aside cash that is equivalent to one month's worth of revenue.

Then, discuss the business continuity plan with your employees. Assign each of them with the roles that they have to play in implementing it. You should designate a place where your staff will gather in case of an emergency as well as giving them a contact number where they can get in touch with you to confirm that they are safe and at the meeting site. Having periodic drills will also help ensure that the plan will be implemented smoothly.

Examples of the drills you can conduct include:

- Launching the business continuity plan. Practice starting up the plan with emphasis on how it will be implemented and the roles that your employees will play
- Data recovery. Back up data and then practice recovering it
- Resuming operations. Test your procedures for restarting the business after the crisis event
- Alternative site exercise. Practice how you will start up operations at your designated alternative site
- Safety exercise. Practice your safety procedures, including evacuation drills and safety confirmation

One last thing to remember is that business continuity plans should not be static. You should review them periodically to ensure that they are still effective. These reviews should be conducted by senior management and should be done at least once a year.

In particular, look at any areas that you may have inadvertently omitted from the plan. Aside from looking at the procedures themselves, you should also consider how the circumstances of your business have changed and how these changes would affect the plan.

Employee Equity Scheme Formation

One way that employers can motivate their employees to perform better and prevent valued ones from leaving is by giving them shares of stock in the company. This not only gives them ownership rights in the company but also entitles them to share in the profits.

There are many reasons why employers would want to share ownership with employees, including:

- As part of an exit plan. If the employer would eventually want to leave the business, and there is no one who is willing or able to take over, the best way of exiting may be to sell it to employees.

- Sharing the responsibilities of running the business. Since an equity scheme gives employees ownership rights, they also effectively become co-runners of the business.

- To raise capital. If you have a promising business model, your employees might be willing to accept a lower salary in exchange for shares in the business. This will free up cash that can be used towards the business' operating expenses or to expand and grow it.

- To help motivate employees. Studies have shown that businesses where the employees are co-owners perform better than companies that are not employee owned.

- To attract or keep valued employees. If an employee is a co-owner, they are more likely to stay.

- To enjoy possible tax benefits. Depending on the laws of your country, the company may enjoy tax breaks if they start an equity scheme. For instance, contributions to buy stock can be tax-deductible.

There are a number of ways that you can create an employee equity scheme, including:

Employee Stock Ownership Plan. This is a benefit scheme in which the assets are invested in company stock, and generally includes all full-time employees who qualify to participate. Under this scheme, the company can acquire shares to distribute to employees by contributing its own shares, contributing money to buy its stock or take out a loan to buy stock, with the company taking care of the repayment. Shares are usually distributed when the employee leaves the company, although some plans may also include provisions for earlier distributions.

Stock Option Plan. This scheme gives employees the right to company stock at a pre-determined price and a specified period. For instance, under the plan the employee may have the option to buy 150 shares at a price of $10 per share. Thus, if the stock price goes up to $15, the employee may choose to exercise their option and buy the 150 shares at $10.

Employee Stock Purchase Plan. Under this scheme, the employee is allowed to buy shares and pay for them through salary deductions. The price of the shares is generally discounted by as much as 15% and the employee can buy at any time during the offering period. The employee can choose to hold on to the shares or sell them, and since they are discounted, they can make a profit even if the share price has gone down.

For small businesses with only up to ten employees where issuing shares might not be feasible, a Phantom Share Plan might be a better alternative. Instead of ownership rights, the employee is entitled to get a cash bonus based on the company's profits. There are two ways you can implement a PSS:

- Profit sharing. The employee receives a bonus based on a percentage of the annual profits and will also receive a share in the profits if the business is sold.

- Improvement shares. The bonus is given based on how much the company's profits have improved above a pre-determined base level.

A CFO can help you to determine which equity best suits your company's particular circumstances, and they can also set it up so that you won't be in violation of any tax laws or legal requirements.

9 FUNNEL ANALYSIS AND MEASURING CONVERSION

Creating a "sales funnel" is essential for those running small businesses since it can spell the difference between success and failure. The sales funnel refers to the process that you lead potential customers through that will hopefully end with them performing a desired action, i.e. making a purchase or signing up for a service.

There are generally five stages in a sales funnel:

Awareness. In this stage, you let potential customers know about the product or service that you offer. There are many ways you can do this. Traditionally companies would place advertisements in newspapers and magazines, or give away fliers. Online businesses have a wider range of options available to them.

For instance, you can optimize your site so that when someone conducts a search using search terms that are in your market niche, a link to your site is one of the top results. You can also create a blog with useful content related to your niche, and then include a link to your business site at the end of the post or through a hyperlink. Basically, your goal at this stage is to drive traffic to your site.

However, you don't just want to just create traffic for traffic's sake. Your goal is to drive potential leads to your site who want to learn more about what you have to offer and how it can help them solve a particular problem that they have.

Interest. In this stage, you tell site visitors what you have to offer to stoke their interest. Thus, when they click on the link, they might land on a landing page that has information about your products or services. Or they might land on a home page that introduces visitors to your company and what it offers.

During this phase, you can also ask visitors to opt-in to a mailing list so that they'll regularly receive newsletters and other updates from you. There are various ways to get customers to opt-in. For instance, you can ensure that the layout of your homepage or landing page is easy to navigate and has attention-grabbing features such as striking headlines and images. You can also ensure that the copy on the homepage or landing page clearly sells your product or service by defining what problem it solves. And, of course, you can ensure that your blog posts have useful and unique content.

A popular method you can use to encourage people to sign-up is to offer them a free eBook or online course. You can use these freebies to create demand for your product or service by introducing them and explaining how they can solve a problem. Include a call to action to encourage them to perform actions such as clicking a link to learn more or to contact your sales department.

Desire. This is the phase just before the customer takes the desired action, when you've already engaged them and you want them to take the next step. You can make them want to buy by making the product or service look attractive through striking photos and descriptions, as well as enumerating the various options available to them. As they become available, you can post customer reviews as well.

You should also include supporting content such as an easy returns policy, free or cheap shipping and extras that they can get. Of course, you can support your sales efforts through your blog posts where you can provide content such as how-to's and tips, then mention your product at the end, with a link if they want to learn more.

Conversion. This is the phase during which the customer takes the desired action. Make sure that at this phase, it is very easy for the customer to perform the action by removing any potential blocks that could cause them to change their minds. For instance, make sure that they can easily place products in their shopping cart and check out. If you want them to sign up for something, ask them for the minimum amount of information and make sure it takes as little time as possible.

Re-engagement. This is the phase that most people creating sales funnels frequently forget. You want people to not just make one purchase from you, but to continue buying in the future. Unless you retain your customers, you will not be able to grow your business since you cannot continue to generate revenue in the future. Essentially, without retention, you will have to keep attracting new customers that you will have to pay to acquire.

The metric used to measure how many customers you lose is called the "churn rate". Customer churn happens when customers stop dealing with a business, for whatever reason. It is important for you to be aware of your churn rate because it is more expensive to acquire new customers than to keep the ones that you already have.

The best way to encourage re-engagement is to create a relationship with your customers. For instance, if they have opted-in to your mailing list, you can send them alerts about new products or services or remind them about the ones that you already have. You can also use the alerts to encourage new sales by offering promotions such as sales or coupons.

But most importantly, make sure that your customers know how much you value their patronage. For instance, after they make a purchase, send them a thank-you email or include a note with their package that thanks them and may include a coupon or other incentive to buy again.

At the same time, however, avoid seeming too needy. For instance, don't bombard your customers with promotional e-mails. If they have not made a purchase for some time, you can send them a message asking how they are and reminding them of what you have to offer. If they don't respond, don't keep sending them messages.

Performing Funnel Analysis

Funnel analysis is a way to study which parts of your sales funnel are the most effective so that you can tweak it and make it more effective. Basically, the way it works is that you break down your funnel into different steps. Each step represents a different page, and then you use a web analytics tool to measure how many users reached each page.

Here are the steps for creating a funnel analysis:

Define the steps in your funnel. To make the analysis more effective, you have to craft your sales funnel in such a way that the users have to go through each step without being able to skip through any of them. For an e-commerce site, for instance, you could have the following steps:

1. Landing Page
2. Clicking on a product
3. Adding the product to the shopping cart
4. Filling up the purchase form
5. Confirming the order
6. Paying for the purchase

To make the analysis more manageable, you should track five to ten steps. If there are certain stages that can be broken down into more steps, you can create a 'sub-funnel' that can be analyzed on its own. For instance, if registering for a service involves several steps, you can analyze this on its own in addition to adding it to the main funnel.

The next step is to choose a tool to conduct your funnel analysis. The easiest way is to use smart tools such as Google Analytics or Mixpanel. However, you can use Excel to create your conversion funnel by drafting the steps on paper and then reproducing them on your spreadsheet. Then import the data from the web analytics tool, either by using an Excel plugin or API.

Now you can visualize your funnel. If you use Google Analytics, you will be provided with a chart that tells you at each stage how many users entered a page, how many exited or were lost and how many proceeded to the next page. If you use Excel, the best and simplest way to visualize your funnel is by using a bar graph, where a bar represents each stage.

The most useful information you can get from funnel analysis is identifying bottlenecks. When you look at a bar chart, you can quickly see which stages experience a serious drop-off. There are some stages where you can expect people to not continue, such as when they are asked to fill in their credit card details. However, there are some stages where you do not expect such drop-offs and so these could be a red flag that there is a bottleneck that needs to be addressed.

CONCLUSION

Thank you for reading. I hope you found it useful.

Any feedback is more than welcome and I look forward to hearing from you if you have any comments or suggestions. And, please feel free to contact me if you would like to learn more about how a CFO can help your business grow.

ABOUT THE AUTHOR

Kyle Brennan is the Founder of Ralston Finance Partners, which delivers flexible finance support and guidance to growing businesses. He serves as Chief Financial Officer at Feeld and advises businesses on how to become more efficient and navigate through stages of expansion. He holds a Masters in Finance and MBA from Creighton University.

Made in United States
North Haven, CT
20 October 2022

25695899R00093